HOW TO ELIMINATE TAX FRAUD, BLACK MONEY, BLACK MARKET, UNDERGROUD ECONOMIES

PROLOGUE

The recent global economic crisis would never have happened if it weren't for tax fraud.

In this book, I demonstrate how to eliminate almost all tax fraud, underground economies, black market and black money by means of existing technologies, with the following list of advantages: the budget deficit would be eliminated with a surplus created that would be used to pay off the debt; some 30 capitalist countries would be able to distribute unemployment benefits equivalent to the average minimum monthly wage, while in other countries where per capita income is lower, money could be channeled into setting up charity canteens and hostels for the poor; pension payments would not come under threat, with the minimum amounts raised; while many social projects could be implemented.

The French economy, for example, is on red alert thanks to the fact that money lost to tax fraud represents 15% of its GDP. This should never have been allowed to be the case. In Italy the figure is 27%, in Spain 25%, in Germany 16%, in the United Kingdom 12.5%, in the United States 8.6%, and in Brazil, 39%.

It would be almost impossible to buy and sell drugs under the system outlined in this book, which also provides solutions on how to prevent kidnappings, illegal immigration, and smuggling, as well as those designed to almost completely eradicate theft and political corruption. Terrorism would also be stamped out, as there would be no agreements to be made with FARC guerrillas, with the same applying to any uprisings against democratic governments. Measures to diminish Islamic terrorism are also provided, as are strategies to greatly reduce theft.

Prisons would be almost empty, as crime would be negligible.

Without tax fraud, individuals and companies who pay the correct amount of tax would benefit through the lowering of both personal income and corporate tax in many countries around the world.

The global crisis is largely due to an ageing population, which has led to a gradual rise in government spending on pensions. Another factor is the budget deficit, which means more money must be spent on paying off interest accumulated on the debt. As these two problems continue to worsen, sooner or later it will become clear that the only solution is the system proposed in this book.

Unless action is taken, communism will spread in capitalist countries, as many businesses and companies will be forced to close, eradicating jobs and creating discontent among the population, leading to the kind of strikes and riots currently affecting Venezuela.

Communism runs against people's natural ambition, hampering production, with the only people it favors those in charge.

Politicians' strategy is to implement ineffective or unjust measures such as raising taxes or social security payments due to the two problems previously cited. Countries such as Denmark have solved the pension problem with the introduction of private plans; however other countries such as Spain, where people receive a lump sum upon retirement and nothing more, are currently running a deficit.

Taxes charged to banks or via healthcare copays draw in hardly any money at all.

No political party has strategies to solve such problems, nor do any of them know how to improve the efficiency of institutions, because they defend different ideologies that aim to control institutions such as unprofitable state-owned enterprises, in order to provide jobs for friends or family, or cover up all sorts of wrongdoing.

With hardly any tax fraud, companies' social security contributions would be reduced, while lowered tax rates would lead to the creation of companies and jobs.

It's more than just lowering taxes, however, because without our system, reducing spending and hoping for growth just like in Ireland would take much longer and only add to the deficit. This is what the economists say, anyway, but it's not a solution like eliminating tax fraud.

The current situation has led to great social tension and violence.

Many administrative staff could be made redundant, which would streamline operations and allow them to receive social security benefits like anyone else currently unemployed. Distributing unemployment benefits would not, however, reduce the tax burden.

In this book we explain how individual and corporate tax declarations would be automatically entered into the system, meaning that individuals, companies, and consultancies would have very little work to do themselves.

Our aim is to make politicians aware – particularly in corrupt countries – that society's most pressing problems may be solved by means of existing technologies.

Another consequence might be that people outside the political sphere – such as is my case – would be inspired to form a political party incorporating all of the ideas and ingenious tricks you are about to read in this book.

It would be advantageous for Europe to eliminate its deficit, paying the debt off over the years and adding to welfare funds. It would also save the European Union. In Spain, for example, the public deficit is growing steadily each year and nobody bats an eyelid because communism is on the rise. Communism resulted in 100 million deaths in the twentieth century and is the worst political system of all. This is also why Greece had to be rescued.

In Latin America, our system would reduce crime and existing poverty.

In the United States, it would solve the problem of illegal immigration and tackle crime, as well as boosting the economy.

It would also prove advantageous for Africa, as the most capitalist countries would have more money to send to the continent as aid, which would also help countries in Asia. The Chinese economy would be boosted, as money lost through tax fraud is equivalent to 11% of the country's GDP.

This book provides serious solutions to political and economic problems faced by the entire capitalist world, employing all of today's existing technologies to do so.

Politicians would not be in favor of the system because it would stop them from embezzling or pocketing public funds, preventing parties from using false invoices.

Prisons would be almost empty, because there would be hardly any crime.

Financial advisors would not like the system either, because with automatic tax declarations, their work would dry up.

Drug addicts would be another group affected, as hardly anybody would be able to get hold of drugs, thanks to how difficult it would be to sell them.

Illegal immigrants would also be against the system, as they would be slaves, either locked up in jail or deported.

The system would be no good for bankers, due to the tight controls placed on banks that would prevent them from accumulating black money in their vaults.

Civil servants would also be strongly against the system, because many would find themselves out of work.

Our system would not be of much interest to debt collectors either, as there would be hardly any debt.

Hardworking employees would, however, be some of the most in favor of the system, as taxes and crime would both fall.

Young people would be behind it because of the unemployment benefits.

More funding could be made available to research, attracting some of our star talents back, meaning leading professors would also be in favor of it.

The unemployed would also support our system, as they would receive unemployment benefits.

Multinational telecommunications companies would also be behind us, because they would be called upon to implement the system and would make a lot of money in the process.

What we need is a change in mentality, which has been attempted many times throughout history. In countries such as the United States, Sweden, Norway, Denmark, France, Germany, and the United Kingdom, etc., the idea that politicians should be honest has been written into the current system. In the UK, for example, a politician was asked to step down due to the discovery that he had paid his gardener with public funds. I have never even heard of the illegal funding of political parties in the United States.

In these countries the system would be highly successful, and as it's already being considered in the United States, Sweden, Denmark, and Norway, these should be the first countries to implement our system.

One country that I believe would be particularly suitable for our system is France, because the majority of rich people are willing to work together to tackle the situation facing the country, agreeing to the raising of taxes. If this went ahead in France and other countries in the European Union, Spain, Italy, and Greece would be next, as these are the EU's most corrupt members, therefore the system would serve as a kind of utopia for them.

My aim is to do away with tax fraud, underground economies, and black money. While writing this book, I realized that kidnappings could also be prevented, illegal immigration clamped down on, and theft reduced, effectively tackling all kinds of crime.

CHAPTER I

The system

Section I.1. A description of the system, its one great trick, and why this doesn't necessarily spell the end for cash

This system for applying effective anti-terrorist measures, preventing theft, and almost completing eliminating tax evasion, underground economies, black money, drug trafficking, kidnappings, illegal immigration, theft, corruption, and smuggling, involves a complete eradication of the circulation of cash among individuals and companies. Cash would only be used among the various banks, which is why it would still exist (although in Denmark they want to get rid of it completely). Using this trick would allow us to eliminate tax fraud and greatly reduce crime. This would come in what I hope will be the near future, in order to fight the growing spread of communism.

The only kind of money in circulation among individuals and companies would be electronic money, with individuals able to make payments both by card and by means of machines able to scan our fingerprints.

Although this book seems somewhat revolutionary, it isn't really, as such a shift began with the advent of the internet. The technology for such a change in society has existed for years, as was mentioned in the prologue, and as many politicians have remarked, despite their failure to implement the change mentioned in this book.

To begin with, let's use this chapter to discuss the enormous advantages and all of the problems associated with this new world. Later, we'll move on to technology and the economy, although details of both will be introduced in previous sections. Finally, we'll move on to consider how a variety of professions would be shaped by this new world.

In order to pay for a product or a service, we would place our index finger on a machine with access to the internet, which would scan our digital fingerprint in order to transfer electronic money from our bank to the bank used by the supplier of the product or service.

This operation would be both extremely fast and applicable to all kinds of businesses.

Once a day, cash would be circulated among the various banks.

Section I.2. The current systems

Denmark is set to completely do away with cash, with the country planning to operate solely on credit cards and bank transfers. Our system is more comprehensive, however, because we would control banks, foundations, and political parties, etc. much more efficiently.

Such tight control would be thanks to a Central Computer that would contain all of the data for the above list, allowing them to be investigated at any moment, as every individual and company would have a single account for income and expenditure.

In Sweden, nowadays, people use credit cards to pay for bus tickets and items in stores, preventing theft. In actual fact, the country would like its entire economy to run off credit cards.

Payment is slower with credit cards, as you have to enter your PIN. If we were to operate exclusively on credit cards, theft would be rife. Our system is superior.

Norway would like to follow Sweden's example, however the people are against it, claiming encroaches on their freedom.

Applying this same line of reasoning would mean that we could inform tax inspectors their investigations were an infringement of our freedom, with the same said about the government's access to our emails and internet browser histories. When considered this way, it becomes clear that all I am suggesting is tighter control.

In September 2014, Venezuela announced that the country's payment system would move to use digital fingerprints; however it is yet to implement this.

The United States is also considering the sole use of credit cards for payment, where people even use credit cards to pay for coffee.

Section I.3. Other systems and several problems with our own

There will, of course, be other systems, such as one using iris recognition (although from my point of view, this would be rather uncomfortable).

Anyone without hands and therefore without fingerprints, could, however, still use our system, because they could still pay by credit card, using a variety of forms of identification, whether their ID card, driver's license or social security card. This is another reason why our system would be more comprehensive than that used in Denmark.

It would be problematic for the visually impaired, however. Perhaps we could use audible signals, such as those used at pedestrian crossings. Or a better solution might be for machines to use voice technology to tell the person how much is to be paid.

The digital fingerprint system is swift, modern, and convenient.

Section I.4. System advantages

The advantages of the system are as follows: there would be practically no tax fraud, underground economies, black money, black market, drug trafficking, theft, or political corruption (merely that among friends or relatives, sometimes even without offices of their own), and hardly any illegal immigration or smuggling, with public debt eliminated in many countries. Anti-terrorist.measures.

The most important thing to be tackled is tax fraud, as it is the basis of our system for a functioning society, via its elimination of the public debt in many capitalist countries in the space of only a few years.

There would very little social security fraud in our system, although not all employees would be in the national fingerprint system. Such people would be illegal immigrants, whom we will later refer to as slaves, and they would only work for food and other minimal costs for business owners. As they wouldn't be paid a salary, they wouldn't cheat the tax office.

There are another three situations that could lead to a negligent amount of fraud that will be discussed in the section on the economy, demonstrating how tax fraud will be almost entirely wiped out.

Purchasing invoices in order to justify expenses would be prohibited, as would the use of inflated invoices.

There would be no counterfeit money in circulation.

In some 30 capitalist countries, unemployment benefits would be provided to people out of work and to people who work part time. In other capitalist countries, such people would receive small sums to buy food and other basic necessities.

Indigenous people would be alcoholics or would suffer from some form of mental illness, but would be looked after.

There would be no black money and no underground economies. In countries in which prostitution is illegal, there would be no black market for weapons or explosives (I'll explain why afterwards).

We would be able to know the whereabouts of anyone to have disappeared through their consumption patterns.

Section I.5. How to prevent kidnappings

As kidnappings involve the transfer of large sums of money to strangers, our computer system would put a stop to them, as it would only allow us to transfer money to close family.

As transfers would be capped at €50 per day, €300 per month, and €3,600 per year to people outside our close family, nobody would get kidnapped over such small amounts of money.

What would be allowed would be transfers between individuals and companies, or between two companies.

If someone were to be kidnapped and ordered to make one of the types of payments cited above, there would always be the possibility that the family of the victim would report it once the victim had been released, with an investigation launched into the company the kidnapper had paid and the items on any bills. This would be extremely risky for kidnappers, preventing them from kidnapping anyone in the first place.

In the case of kidnappings involving large payments made between companies, the kidnappers' company would make so much money that they would be investigated for fraud, with the company forced to pay the ransom also recording plummeting revenue, which would also be investigated.

Only the government would be able to pay kidnappers. If jihadi terrorists were to kidnap three Spanish journalists, for example, the government would pay the ransom, which would be a very bad thing as this money could be used to cause further damage.

Section I.6. How to greatly reduce theft

There would be hardly any theft, because if our television set were stolen from our home, for example, it would be almost impossible for the thief to sell it on due to the controlling of items and stock. Bartering would not be allowed, as figures for the consumption of basic items would be inordinately high or low.

It would be impossible to steal cash, as it would all be with the banks.

Theft would therefore shift to items of personal use. To use the TV set as an example, if I didn't have one, I might steal one from someone else's house, meaning that theft would be reduced to basic necessities and would make little impact in the 30 countries to adopt our system.

Food in supermarkets could also be stolen, as could clothes from large warehouses, however this would only occur in less capitalist countries, as in our system the unemployed would receive benefits.

Nowadays you can't steal luxury cars and smuggle them off to Africa, as cars have a GPS system and are easy to locate, although some people might know how to tamper with the effectiveness of such GPS systems.

Highly valuable jewels could be stolen and transported to countries without our system in place. Jewelers' security systems would therefore have to be improved, while people who keep a lot of jewelry at home would have to transfer it to safes.

Section I.7. How to minimize political corruption

There wouldn't be much political corruption either, as all transactions would be recorded, meaning any kickbacks would be registered in the system and denied if the recipient was not a member of the sender's immediate family.

It would be prohibited to transfer money to people outside our immediate family or to political parties, unless we were a member, and even then, we would only be allowed to transfer restricted amounts.

The main advantage of this is that it would do away with the modern exchange of cash, which cannot be controlled.

Corruption may occur if people appoint friends or relatives to political posts.

The worst form of corruption would be inflated pricing, such as items worth €10 being sold at €15 with €2 going to a politician, for example. This could only be done with relatives, however, except we wouldn't charge the extra €2 mentioned.

It would be completely prohibited to give gifts over a certain value to people outside our family, with studies required to fix such values. Gifts could be exchanged between couples, for example, as long as they were of a low value, unless such couples lived together in common-law partnerships, in which case they would be allowed to exchange any gifts they want.

Section I.8. The main reason why there would be hardly any tax fraud, underground economies, black market or black money

The main reason is that the country's entire economy would be controlled, as would company stock and maximum profit thresholds, with money transfers highly restricted, etc.

There would be no black money, because cash would be held in banks, and would not circulate among companies and individuals.

Section I.9. How to reduce crime

Crime would be greatly reduced under our system because everybody would be able to pay for things, whether by means of their salary or unemployment benefits, which would lead to less conflict between married couples.

Under our system, crime would only involve psychopaths, misogynists, and assassins, although it would be impossible to completely eradicate (due to such tendencies being innate to some personalities, particularly those with a specific DNA sequence).

Section I.10. How to prevent smuggling

Tobacco smuggling would be banned, because tobacco would only be sold in specialist stores and bars, so that the police could control such a trade. All smuggled products would lead to the company selling them on exceeding their maximum profit threshold, which would spur an investigation.

Stock would be controlled with all sales and purchases recorded, making smuggling much more difficult.

Smugglers would not be able to use machines to charge payments either, and any machines used belonging to other companies would see all movements recorded on the system and studied at a later date.

Smuggling would be reduced to minimal levels. As with drugs, neither of these types of crime would occur at significant levels in countries to implement our system.

Section I.11. Police

When a criminal is wanted by the police – whether a tourist whose visa has expired or a terrorist – any attempts to spend money would see their account frozen, leaving them without anywhere to stay (apart from friends' houses).

The Municipal Computer would investigate the spending of the criminals' friends, which would lead to the criminals themselves.

The few police officers required by the system could patrol the streets as in times past, or take care of the few remaining illegal activities.

Another advantage of our system would be that anyone to have forgotten their ID card could ask the police to use a special machine able to recognize our digital fingerprint. This would also show if we were currently sought by the police or not.

For foreigners from countries which also use our system, we would be able to communicate with other Central Computers in order to determine if such foreigners were criminals.

Section I.12. Tackling drug trafficking

There would be hardly any drug trafficking, because drug traffickers would have no way of charging via the digital fingerprint system, meaning there would be hardly any drugs either. Any drug use would be minimal and wholly personal, such as the cultivation of cannabis plants.

Some people believe that drugs such as cannabis should be legalized, as is the case in the Netherlands (when purchased from authorized sellers). Legalizing hard drugs would not be convenient because healthcare costs would soar as a result.

Any companies attempting to sell drugs would be caught by the Treasury, as a revision of their balance sheets would show income disproportionate to the goods sold, with an inspection performed by plainclothes officers. Inspectors could also investigate a company's items and stock.

A profit rate would be set for every company, representing the relationship between its income and expenditure, with the company prohibited from exceeding this rate. The Treasury would determine this rate for all types of business, with any companies exceeding it investigated and subject to a hefty fine.

Any business found to be selling drugs would be closed down, with the perpetrators imprisoned for drug trafficking, meaning that the few benefits associated with selling drugs would not be worth the risk. Major drug traffickers would therefore be forced to move to another country in which our system is not in use, saving us the headache.

In countries in which prostitution is legal, drugs could be sold, however such sales would be registered in the system, meaning that investigations into drug addicts would analyze their purchases. If various drug addicts were revealed to be buying from the same company, we could monitor such company's activities or conduct a raid of the premises.

In my view, prostitution is the greatest threat to the system's tackling of crime, as sex workers would be able to charge for their services using payment machines and would be able to sell arms and explosives.

This would form a kind of black market. To make all of this a little more palatable, profit on the services provided would have to be restricted, making luxury prostitution illegal.

Despite the fact that it is the oldest profession in the world, prostitution is illegal in Spain, except in strip clubs where the girls consent to it and are given contracts as restaurant servers. Sex work in residential buildings is not monitored, as it's advertised and also consented to.

You also wouldn't be able to transfer money to anyone outside your immediate family; however you would be able to give such family members both money and goods.

Section I.13. How to prevent illegal immigration

There would be hardly any illegal immigration, because foreigners would only be able to spend long periods of time in other countries if on working or student visas.

Foreigners on vacation would only be able to use credit or debit cards, with all businesses forced to charge payments by means of these cards.

The Central Computer would know how long tourists have spent in the country, locating and expelling them (unless they are from the European Union and are in another country in the European Union). Credit and debit cards could also be deactivated, forcing tourists to leave, with the Central Computer freezing their spending upon registering that they are wanted by police.

Other cards could not be used because you would have to declare which card you were going to use upon entry. This card would be registered in the Central Computer by means of communication at border controls.

Another form of control would be to take the fingerprints associated with current accounts at border points, registering in the Central Computer the amount of money in the person's account and adding it to our system servers. Upon leaving the country, such information would be wiped. This would mean that while in the country, foreigners would be treated like citizens.

With our system, illegal immigrants would have no payment machines, so they would not be able to sell anything, and would also not be in the fingerprint system, meaning they couldn't buy anything either.

Africans of unknown origin would be imprisoned and made to work, with any resistance seeing them sent back to where they came from. In prison, however, they would undergo training courses to develop skills to be used whenever they return home.

One solution to try to avoid such imprisonment would be to check which countries such immigrants are from, however this would require more cooperation from Africa in order to be truly viable. In return, the continent would have a digital record of its populations' fingerprints.

The Central Computers for the various African countries could be accessed from any other country by satellite, allowing us to deport suspects upon checking their fingerprints.

Fingerprints might be destroyed by removing fingers or burning them with acid, and in such cases we would imprison perpetrators until they revealed their country of origin.

The only way of surviving would be to work in return for food and accommodation without any disposable income, which would lead people to want to move to other countries, rather than live like slaves.

This entire slavery system would be heavily controlled, just like for prostitutes who are not registered in the fingerprint system.

Anybody running forced-labor rings would be detected due to their elevated expenditure on food, clothing, and accommodation, etc., spurring investigation by the Central Municipal Computer. Perhaps a single slave would not be detected, but several would undoubtedly raise alarm bells.

Anyone keeping slaves would be imprisoned for many years.

The majority of African immigrants are poorly educated and operate in underground economies, therefore they must be fed and trained in their countries of origin, making it better for them not to leave in the first place.

Such training would be given in Africa by means of NGOs; therefore the government would have to donate more money to NGOs such as the Red Cross or Caritas Internationalist.

Illegal immigration would be easier to tackle in the United States.

With the use of all of the measures cited, fences would not be required.

Section I.14. Anti-terrorism measures

Jihadist terrorism is funded by gold, kidnapping and artworks, with such extremists able to buy a wide variety of arms from countries where our system is not in place.

Although the arms trade would be controlled, terrorists could still steal weapons, or attack us physically or with knives.

Our system could also prevent the manufacture of explosives; however terrorists would just import them from other countries that don't use our system.

In countries to have adopted our system, the sale of tanks and heavy arms to terrorist groups would be forbidden. With the eradication of the black market and FARC members being hunted down and captured, terrorists wouldn't be able to buy any kind of arms or ammunition, so such groups would actually disband without us even having to reach an agreement with them, because rather than being terrorists, they would be just like an army with no cash to spend. They would also not be able to buy arms by means of bank transfer, and would be treated by our system as illegal immigrants. The same would apply to any terrorist or army adopting an anti-governmental stance in countries to have implemented our system.

Spanish terrorist group ETA has all but disappeared. If it were to resume its former activities, it would use the companies it runs to acquire credit cards, withdrawing cash and buying arms from the black market in countries which don't follow our system, transporting these arms by means of any system except air travel. ETA is not an army like FARC, and for this reason cannot be completely stamped out.

There would be no way to prevent employees on vacation in a country which doesn't use our system from purchasing arms, as terrorists run companies in which their employees belong to the terrorist group, with such employees therefore able to use credit cards, as only credit cards belonging to tourists illegally in a country would be frozen, whether they are wanted or to have been arrested by the police or Interpol.

Ideas do not just vanish into thin air, but we can protect ourselves by minimizing them with better land and sea controls. Nazism still exists, for example.

We cannot completely get rid of the mafia either, as it can threaten companies by forcing them to buy its products, provided maximum profit thresholds are not exceeded. Money that cannot be earned by blackmailing companies could be earned by raising product prices. Any terrorist group can behave like the mafia.

The mafia could, however, be tracked online by means of consumption patterns, with friends also identifiable by means of their purchases in various establishments.

Section I.15. Our system and security

The head of our system would be a wholly incorruptible man. If the Pentagon were broken into, intruders would be able to access and damage our system, just like modern computer viruses.

There are online systems that have never been hacked; therefore we would employ the security methods used to protect such systems.

Apart from viruses, we would also remove any system for spying on the contents of the Central Computer.

It would be a risk to have just one single Central Computer, because it could break down and become infected with a virus, therefore we would need to have a reserve in place.

Section I.16. The Central Computer, electronic money, and the bunker

The system would require a Central Computer that would control all proceedings in the bunker. We would of course use the best computer in the world, able to process a thousand billion operations per second.

All banks would be represented in the bunker.

Electronic money transfers would produce a daily deficit and surplus of the money held by the respective banks, meaning that cash would have to be physically shifted from one bank to another in the bunker.

A deficit or surplus would be produced for all of the banks because people spend money, and in many cases this means transferring funds from one bank to another, with transfers executed in the following way: if a bank has to send money it would be transferred by means of machines to a specific room in the bunker, and if a bank has a surplus, it would automatically withdraw money from this room. Obviously we would operate with bills and very little money in coins. Bills could be made for amounts up to €10,000.

The Central Computer would record whether a bank is running a deficit or a surplus of our money at the end of the day, due to the fact that all individuals and companies would have a single current account linked to a particular bank for their income and expenditure. Companies, for example, could also only use a single account with a single bank for these operations, using other banks merely for accumulating profit.

To ensure efficient investigation and the smooth running of our system, credit cards would only be linked to current accounts with digital fingerprints attached to them.

The online system would show if any bank were to run out of money. In this case, national banks could borrow from the county's own bank (which would also be in the bunker), which would be highly robust under our system. For international banks, money from abroad would be transferred by airplane to the bunker, because one country might be running low on cash while another is accumulating it.

In order to ensure the money arrived on time, a minimum threshold would to be set for each bank to warn it when funds were running low.

All of these measures would have the added advantage of ensuring that banks would not be able to provide false data for acquiring capital on the stock market.

Section I.17. Operation methods

Our entire system would operate by means of the internet, with payment machines communicating with the servers. The Central Computer would store the data in the servers.

Cell phones nowadays are often connected to the internet, meaning it would not be too much of a stretch for payment machines to also go online.

Other cell phones are also able to read our digital fingerprints, meaning that only the owner can use the phone. Payment machines could use the same technology.

The payment machine would be like a cell phone, meaning it would be highly portable.

The biggest advantage for supermarkets, bars or any other businesses would be that no change would be required.

By using the internet, most of the data would be stored in the Central Computer as it is uploaded from the servers. The servers would need to be extremely fast in order to efficiently locate our digital fingerprint.

We have already said that the information would be uploaded to the servers in a matter of seconds, and once this data were transferred to the Central Computer, it would be erased from the servers, except in the case of standing data, to be discussed in another section.

Payment machines would register tax ID numbers, whether for freelancers or corporations, etc.

Machines would be provided by the Treasury and returned by mail when companies are closed down, when they would be sent on to other freelancers or corporations upon reprogramming.

The Treasury would not charge anything for these machines, as it would be making more money due to eradicating tax fraud thanks to everything being properly registered.

Section I.18. Children, teenagers, and death

Adults would have their fingerprints linked to a current account with a single bank for their income and expenditure.

Children's spending would have to be monitored; therefore they would not be entered into the digital fingerprint system until they come of age. Children's fingers also grow from the ages of 7 to 14, which would be another complication.

Children would have a card similar to the debit cards used by adults, with this card stating the ID number of a parent or guardian, in order to transfer any debt accumulated.

Special ATMs would allow parents or first-degree relatives to enter a child's card in order for them to transfer money from their current account to the child's card. The parent or relative would enter their fingerprint and the child's card into the machine, with only first-degree relatives applicable, otherwise almost anybody could give children money.

All transfers from family members would be made from the account linked to their fingerprint and not from any other account, with "donation to a family member" added for reference.

The ATM would charge a fee of 0.5% of the money transferred to the child.

Such ATMs would not be used for transfers to children over 14, as they would be able to open their own accounts under the supervision of a guardian, with the guardian or other relatives making transfers. In this case, the child would be able to top up their card at any ATM.

This system would work like special internet cards, allowing children to make purchases, and would be of particular use when they are in another part of the country or abroad.

Children over the age of 14 in other countries would be able to open current accounts on their own, as there would be international agreements in place allowing them to do so. Younger minors could also have current accounts linked to a guardian abroad.

When money is transferred to a child, the system would register this as just another transfer, with the amount able to exceed €50 due to the fact that it involves a family member.

Each child would start out with 2 cards, in order that if one were lost, they would be able to use the second card until the Treasury sent out a replacement, however the money on it would be lost. The cards would require the use of a PIN, to prevent use by anyone other than the minor.

Whenever the minor spends money, they would be able to see their card balance in order to control their own spending. If they didn't have enough money to pay for something, information would be extracted from the relevant parent or guardian's account, transferring the payment to this account. This would be automatic, as the card would contain the guardian's national ID number. As a punishment and to prevent this situation from reoccurring, the minor's account would be frozen for 48 hours.

It would be preferable for children not to use their card until they have a good reason to, at around the age of 7. Up to this age, parents would pay for any products children need, as it is not normal to leave children under 7 alone.

When teenagers travel to countries in which our system is not in place, they would be able to withdraw cash in the local currency from ATMs, as their cards would be similar to those used for internet banking. Cards would have to be topped up before travel, just like the schemes for special internet cards.

Anyone turning 18 would get their own current account opened linked to their fingerprint, which would be different from the one set up at 14, as this time no guardian would be linked to the account.

The card would be set up with a single bank, transferring all of the money on the previous card, which would be duly canceled, before registering the new current account with the ID department. The ID department would then add the new account to the Central Computer's database, along with the fingerprint and the amount of money in the account.

The fingerprint would be entered into the system by means of fiber-optic telecommunications between the ID department and the Central Computer. The new account would also record all of the information on the individual's family members.

The servers would be updated with all of the information on those new to the system by the Central Computer.

Those in employment would have enough money to cover their own expenses; otherwise close relatives would make transfers to the account.

The same would happen whenever anyone moves to a new municipality, with the system registering the new address, etc.

In countries in which minors were eligible to work, the company would be able to transfer the monthly salary, as long as it was registered with the Central Computer.

When minors spend money, companies would receive this as income, however such spending would not be reconciled on their accounts, as minors do not file annual tax declarations.

Whenever someone dies, their information would be wiped from the servers, with their fingerprint and family ties also removed. This would ensure that the fingerprint system would work as smoothly as possible.

Inheritances would work the same as they do now. Money and property would be distributed according to the instructions left in the will, paying the fees required to the Treasury. These payments would be made by means of the Central Computer to the country's national bank.

Section I.19. Traveling abroad

When traveling abroad, we would require money in the local currency, but this currency could not be used at home. The solution would be for us to use our credit card to withdraw money from ATMs in the local currency of countries where our system is not in place.

If a country were to adopt our system, we could use our fingerprints to pay for things and wouldn't have to withdraw cash, just like at home.

It would be very convenient for ATMs to be located in airports or hotels abroad, allowing you to withdraw money in the local currency the moment you arrive on foreign soil.

Section I.20. Problems with foreigners remaining in other countries

Foreigners with employment contracts or who are students may have their fingerprints incorporated into the system; however they would first have to open a bank account for their income and expenditure. They would then be able to register for further systems, such as the social security system, and would also receive a special foreigners' ID card.

Foreigners over the age of 18 entitled to unemployment benefits would be removed from the system once these run out, and would have to return to their country of origin due to their inability to make purchases. Any money in their bank account could be transferred at any moment to an account in their country of origin via internet banking.

For students, fingerprints would be removed from the system once they have finished their studies or if they drop out of their course and fail to find work within 6 months.

Foreigners would have to provide information on all family members in order to facilitate bank transfers.

Students would also have to provide details on first-degree family members, so that they could also receive transfers.

Section I.21. Transfers between individuals, banks, and companies

In order to make payments, we would be able to transfer money from any bank linked to our fingerprint to a company with another bank by using a code generated by a system server.

This will be discussed in more detail later on in the book. It would be particularly relevant to imports, exports, and payments that are not up-front, because transport is often outsourced. The main advantage would be the lack of debts.

In having different current accounts, I would be able to use the internet to transfer money to the account linked to my fingerprint. These other accounts could be used to transfer money to the account linked to the fingerprint, or to increase our business or company capital.

Unlimited amounts of money could be transferred between different accounts. It would be prohibited, however, to transfer money in order to pay bills from other accounts, as the system would detect this, due to its inability to locate the two accounts in the servers.

The servers in our system would allow for transfers between accounts as long as both accounts were for income and expenditure. There would be no point opening other accounts and paying fees to keep them open, however they would not be prohibited as they would show up in the bank's server and the system would detect that they belonged to the same person or company.

Our bank's online system would only allow us to accept a transfer from abroad if it were made to an account for income and expenditure, as the servers would have a database for all current accounts linked to our fingerprint. The IBAN code would show which country the transfer was from, which would be useful if we were paid for work done for a client in another country.

In order to be paid while abroad, we would have to have a fixed residence in the country, otherwise this would constitute a criminal activity.

The Central Computer would be linked to the Department of Labor, sharing information on companies' employment contracts, as well as the number of employees, in order that employees could be paid by their employers via any of the system servers.

The Department of Labor would register new employees with the Central Computer, which would then register this information across all of the various servers in the country.

Employees would automatically receive their salaries on a daily basis. Tax retentions for both individuals and companies would also be performed on a daily basis, as would social security withholding.

Transfers exceeding €50 a day to individuals who are not close family would not be permitted, with such quantities only for payment to companies. The same would happen if an individual were to receive over €300 per month in transfers or €3,600 per year from a variety of senders, as they could be selling drugs, unless these payments were from businesses such as stamp collectors, casinos or racecourses, etc., which would be revealed upon investigation.

According to the Civil Registry Office, every individual has first-degree family members, to which they would be able to transfer unlimited amounts of money.

The Civil Registry Office would be linked to the Central Computer, in order that couples getting married would have their data updated to reflect this new relationship as first-degree family members, with the husband able to transfer money to his wife, and vice versa. The same would be permitted among in-laws, nieces and nephews and aunts and uncles, etc.

The Civil Registry Office would send information to the Central Computer on the new configuration of these close family members, with the Central Computer registering this information on all of the national servers.

Divorce would not invalidate the defining of such relationships as "close", however it would be prohibited to lend more than €50 to your former husband or wife. The former couple could remain friends, however in the eyes of the law, they would no longer be husband and wife. Payments to the value of those ruled in the divorce courts would be allowed, with any amounts exceeding these values prohibited.

The Central Computer would be automatically informed of how much a particular party is to receive in alimony, with this money provided for them if the other party cannot pay it.

The Civil Registry Office would register all divorces on the Central Computer.

Common-law couples would be able to send each other money; however payments could not be made to each of the couple's families, as legally they are not defined as "close family".

Section I.22. The payment system for freelancers and employees

A card system similar to that used for children would apply to freelancers and employees.

Payments would be made using cards linked to the company's corporate tax ID, allowing it to make bank transfers as though it were a virtual fingerprint, although expenses would be deductible. The only information required would be the corporate tax number and the branch ID, as the servers would already contain the information on the company current account.

Cards would not have money on them like the ones used for children, and would only feature the corporate tax ID and the branch number, in the case of companies with different offices located around the country. This would be useful for multinationals, for example.

When opening a business or company, the Treasury would register the new data with the Central Computer by creating a website for the company accounts.

In order to prevent people stealing company cards for personal use, cards would be linked to employees' fingerprints, with payment machines checking their validity.

The system would also have to account for employees that are dismissed and those whose contracts are not renewed, or for anyone who loses their card, by creating backup cards, just like spare sets of car keys, although it would be best if this backup card was only used until a new one was sent out. Both the original and the backup card would use the same code, meaning that employees to have been dismissed would have both cards canceled.

These cards would be provided by the Treasury, and would be linked to a code reflecting whether the card has been activated or not. When contracts are terminated, the Treasury would deactivate the card, as it would if the employee were to commit a criminal offense.

Cards would not be returned to the Treasury, because in some places people only work summers, for example. Servers in tourist resorts would, therefore, have their card reactivated each summer.

Cards would be deactivated by means of email, attaching the dismissal letter or sending it via fax. Treasury staff would deactivate cards, removing the person's employment status on the Department of Labor's database.

Company cards would be valid in foreign countries that also use our system. This would be useful for business trips in which employees must pay for gasoline, meals, and accommodation, etc., as these expenses would be deductible.

For employees traveling to countries where our system is not in place, company cards would be no use whatsoever. However the company credit card could be used, as it would register expenses with the company bank, such as those spent on accommodation, for example.

Section I.23. PayPal and other online payment systems

Monitoring would be required for the PayPal system, whereby current accounts linked to email addresses are used to make payments to other email addresses, also linked to current accounts.

The only information available to us is the email address of those sending or receiving money, but not their bank. This online system is more secure than credit cards, however it is also (4%) more expensive.

All sales and purchases made using PayPal would have to be registered with the Central Computer, in order for it to manage our accounts and those of the companies we buy from. The bank to which our PayPal account is linked would automatically register all of our incoming and outgoing PayPal transfers to the servers, in order for this information to be communicated to the Central Computer.

Some people might use this system to sell items without a license. Any income exceeding the cap of €300 per month would be blocked by the system, saving on investigation costs.

This would not prevent people from selling on their old movies and magazine back editions, etc.

Anyone receiving over €300 in income per month would have to register as a company. Income under €300 per month could constitute tax fraud if more money is made legally, with tax to be paid to the Treasury.

For systems such as Western Union, individuals would only be able to send money to first-degree family members whenever the quantity exceeds €300 per month. We could also send money to a company by means of Western Union in order to purchase its products. Western Union would therefore require close monitoring, with its incoming and outgoing payments automatically uploaded to a system server

Online payment systems would operate in almost the same fashion as credit or debit cards have up until now, with the Central Computer informed of the details of all transactions just like with the PayPal system.

Apart from online, people would only be allowed to use credit cards when they have run out of money or when abroad on vacation. The slight fluctuations produced by the monitoring of items will be discussed later on in this book.

Section I.24. The main problem with our system

The main obstacle to the global implementation of our system are the divisions between people.

Our system could be implemented among countries with strong currencies, such as those using the US dollar, the pound, or the euro, for example.

A currency's value can plummet due to the irresponsibility shown by the country in question. When Fidel Castro came to power, for example, he was informed that the problem with Cuba was that there was no money, so money was printed and inflation duly soared.

One solution would be to set up international commissions in the IMF to ensure this does not occur, as the same thing happened years ago in Argentina, and this is not to mention single currencies.

Due to the absence of borders, the system could not be set up for each individual country in the Euro zone, as credit cards could not be used. This is because the system requires us to indicate which credit card we intend to use when crossing the border.

Individual systems could be set up for countries in the Americas, as these countries use different currencies.

In the future there would be a single currency, perhaps known as the Bitcoin. George Soros has spent years arguing for the existence of a single currency.

Another solution would be to return to using the gold standard.

CHAPTER II

Technology

Section II.1. Payment machines

Payment machines would have to issue invoices and receipts; therefore they would be equipped with keyboards and a small printer. Keyboards would feature screens, just like those used on cell phones.

Plumbers would use payment machines with specially-designed programs, for example. These would feature item codes, with the plumber typing in the item and the system searching for it, just like using Google, where you type in an item and select what you are looking for among the search results.

We would be able to register prices different to those pre-programmed on the machine given to us by the Treasury; however they would have to adhere to our maximum profit thresholds.

Depending on a company's corporate activities, payment systems would use different programs, although the machine itself would very often be the same.

Machines would be updated online with details of new items the same way that antivirus software is updated, with updates varying between trades and companies.

We would also have to scan barcodes such as European Article Numbers (EANs), which are used by businesses such as supermarkets.

Printers would be small, issuing receipts with the corporate tax ID number, the items on the bill, and our own corporate tax ID or individual ID number.

There would be no need for a machine or computer to register the bank used for the transaction, because a company's accounts could be consulted by means of a cell phone with an internet connection.

Section II.2. Invoices and receipts

Invoices would be printed on paper and registered internally by the payment machine, detailing all items and the total value to be paid for the customer's reference.

Once the customer has paid with their company card, the receipt would be printed and shown to be the same as the written invoice. The only thing left to do would be to upload it to a server in our system.

Section II.3. How to prevent war breaking out between banks

Legislation would be required to ensure that commission charged by banks in our system would be standardized, to ensure banks would not compete in order to attract customers.

Banks would neither pay nor charge for transfers made in the system worth less than €100, for example.

Section II.4. The different types of payment machines

The machines described would be used by businesses in general, except stamp collectors, racecourses, and lotteries, etc., as in these cases the machines would have to pay us instead.

Drugstores and non-profit associations would also require different machines, as will be discussed later on in this book.

All companies paying us by means of the fingerprint system would be allowed to pay out over €50 per day. A stamp collector that wants to purchase our collection, for example, would have a code for all payments for accounting purposes.

When paying someone who lives in a country where our system has not been adopted, a payment machine would be used along with a credit or debit card.

Such machines could be designed so that they could accept card payments and pay us too.

Other machines could also be designed so that companies could pay us in 30, 60, or 90 days, or whatever the period agreed to by the two parties.

There would be a special button indicating the number of days. Once the period had elapsed, the Central Computer would charge the amount automatically.

Each company would request the number of machines it requires from the Treasury, with all machines interconnected and linked to an online company network.

Section II.5. The Central Computer and the servers

As previously stated, the Central Computer would have to be particularly fast in order to efficiently update all of the information contained on it.

The entire system would be set up using servers, just like the internet, and these would be located in secure locations fitted with security cameras to prevent vandalism.

If a server were to break down, it would be repaired or replaced and the information transferred to another server in our system. All of a country's servers would be connected by means of fiber optics.

As all companies would have Wi-Fi, payment machines would use fiber optics to communicate to the nearest server the company's corporate tax IDs and branch number, along with our fingerprint and the total amount to be paid, which would in turn locate our current account.

Special machines that charge after periods of 30 or 60 days, etc., would also upload this information. The number of days an invoice could be paid, for example, would also be registered.

This would be a similar process to that used by cell phones connected to the internet. The difference would be that cell phones select a server that communicates with the server hosting a website, making this a lengthier process than our system, and also meaning a lot of information must be downloaded.

Under our system, once a fingerprint has been located, we would then be sent the data registered in the server in order for the payment to be authorized, along with our name and ID number. We would not be informed of corporate tax numbers as this information is linked to company cards.

Cell phones can sometimes connect very quickly to the internet even without Wi-Fi access, however reception may be patchy. For this reason, as previously stated, all companies would be obligated to install a Wi-Fi network.

Section II.6. Servers and standing data

At the beginning of the process, the Central Computer would be informed of personal data such as our fingerprint, the widest part of our fingerprint, our name and address, postal code, our international ID number, and the bank account chosen for our income and expenditure with our fingerprint linked to it. It would also be provided with information on our first-degree family members and their international IDs if over the age of 18. In the case of children over the age of 7, their ID card details would be registered, as would the bank account details of children who are first-degree relatives, as would a list of all the associations we belong to, the maximum amount of money we are allowed to donate to these associations, and a code indicating if we are wanted by police or have been arrested. The system would also be informed of data on our debit and credit cards. All of this would be registered for every individual.

Donations made by members of an association would be limited according to type. A tennis club is not the same as a political party, for example. The Treasury would set limits in each case.

Companies would have to register their international corporate tax ID, address, postal code, bank account, email account for correspondence, and commercial activities (in order to calculate deductible expenses), code for the company type so that all of its stock may be located, international individual IDs for all employees so that their transfers may be authorized, and company cards with codes indicating whether or not they have been activated.

If a company operates across various branches or is a multinational, these branches would be registered as though separate although would use the same bank account and corporate tax ID. Cards belonging to employees in the different areas would all contain the branch code in order that they could all be located by our system server.

In such cases, the server would register the corporate tax ID plus the number of the branch. Company websites would show the accounts information for the branches and the invoices to be paid. At the end of the tax year, the accounts would be done for the company as a whole.

Children's cards would also constitute standing data.

When a company card is destroyed, it would also be removed from the server, which would also happen when a child turns 18.

All of the item codes for the different types of business and current accounts for NGOs and non-profit organizations would also constitute standing data.

All of the streets in a country and their respective postal codes would be another form of standing data.

Section II.7. Tricks for improving the system

We would not connect to the bank directly, as it would have to connect to the Central Computer, which would require two separate connections and render the system somewhat unintelligent.

The reality is that we would indeed connect to all of the banks in order to provide an influx of information from each of the Municipal Computers to the various bank branches, which would be useful for people who don't have internet access and also indispensable to the branches' monitoring of their transactions.

To make the system more efficient, every server would store the fingerprints of everyone aged 18 or over living in the country, meaning we wouldn't need the server to connect with the Central Computer every time a payment is made.

Another trick would be for supermarkets and bars to have enough memory on their payment machines to be able to save the fingerprints of their regular customers and the information on them in the server, meaning the server wouldn't have to look up our fingerprint every time we make a transaction.

It would be just like paying with a bank card, but even faster because the server wouldn't need to look anything up, as this information would be directly attached to our international ID code, already registered by the server on our system. The payment machine would save our fingerprint and ID number. If paying by card, no information would need to be saved.

This concept does require tweaking, however. In theory, a database would be created of customers that have only purchased items from a business once, with the ID of anyone going on to make a second purchase on the same day already in the system.

If a customer does not return within 2 months, their data would be removed from the database. If a customer has purchased items in a store on 3 separate days, their data would be added to the customer data section, which the payment machine would use to look up their fingerprint. This would be faster than using a server, as the machine wouldn't have to scan as many fingerprints.

If a customer does not return within 2 months, the payment machine would assume that they are no longer a regular customer, or that they have died, automatically removing them from the customer database.

We would use the following trick to make it easier for the server to locate a customer's fingerprint. First we would consult the fingerprints of the residents of the same street in which the business is located, as the server would store the business's corporate tax ID (and branch number, if applicable), allowing it to locate the company address.

If the server cannot find a fingerprint registered for the same street, it would then scan adjacent streets, followed by nearby cities, then the local province, and then nearby provinces, meaning it wouldn't have to scan all of the fingerprints registered in the server in our system.

This feature would organize searches according to postal codes. Once a company's postal code has been located, fingerprints in the surrounding streets would be searched. It would be easier if every street had its own postal code.

Section II.8. The Central Computer's robot system

The Central Computer's robot system would update all of the information on the servers.

If, for example, we were to begin the day with €1,000 in the bank account linked to our fingerprint or our company, and then spent €10, this would be permitted by the server because €10 is less than the €1,000 with which we began the day, with the server registering this expenditure of €10 and the €1,000 we had at the beginning of the day.

For the recipient of the payment, the server would register this payment and the previous amount the recipient had in their account.

The Central Computer's robot system would therefore rapidly upload all of our expenses to the Central Computer.

If we were to spend €10, for example, all of the national servers would register our new balance of €990, with this operation known as a system "refresh".

The refresh would also store our data on our website, placing us in communication with the servers that store the websites, allowing us to search for information more efficiently. Data would thus be duplicated, stored on both the Central Computer and on our website if fluctuations have occurred when it was refreshed.

Transfers would also be taken into account when the system refreshes, as would the incorporation of new fingerprints, changes to addresses or banks, the removal of the deceased, and the adding and removing of employee data.

Satellites allow data to be transmitted at a maximum of 8 megabytes per second, with copper allowing for 1 gigabyte per second, and fiber optics 10 gigabytes per second. The data used to store incoming payments and expenditure would be as follows:

4 bytes: the number on a company invoice.

4 bytes: the date (1 byte for the year, 1 byte for the hour, 1 byte for the minute and 1 byte for the second).

4 bytes: The code generated by the server for the payment of the corresponding transaction.

1 byte: The code for expenditure by foreigners or minors so that such expenditure does not enter into the accounts system.

4 bytes: The amount on the invoice.

4 bytes: The amount of the deductible expense.

1 byte: The code for the standard chart of accounts.

6 bytes: For international corporate tax IDs or individual ID numbers, four for the number (including that of the branch), one for the national numerical code, and one more for the letter in numerical form, in order to allow the server to register this on the system.

6 bytes: The international corporate tax IDs or individual ID numbers associated with incoming or outgoing payments. For security reasons, this would be useful for accounting purposes (as will be discussed in the financial section).

1 byte: The numerical code for the corresponding VAT or any other tax to be paid if the country is not part of the European Union, which the Central Computer would be able to identify due to the amount of the tax paid.

2 bytes: The number of days in which the invoice must be paid.

1 byte: The number of months in which the invoice must be paid.

6 bytes: The number on any debit or credit card belonging to foreigners in the country as tourists, with this information uploaded to the server by border control. In the European Union, all Central Computers and servers would store this information.

This gives a total of 44 bytes, meaning sending or receiving payments would require very little data storage on the system.

To give an idea of just how fast fiber-optic technology works, a grand total of 204 million payments would be registered per second. As every payment would be duplicated for the sender and the recipient, this would mean 102 million invoices per second.

In actual fact, the number would be lower due to invoices between banks exceeding €100 and involving different banks. Transfers between banks will be discussed later on in this book.

The system would be refreshed by means of Intermediate Computers located every 100 km or every 300 square km. These areas are not wholly exact, merely representing a strategy to be adapted to the size of the population covered.

Different areas could be used in Russia. Siberia, for example, is sparsely populated; therefore one Intermediate Computer could be located every 300 km or even further apart. The Moscow area would be more suited to 100 km stretches, with the Intermediate Computer located in the city.

The system would be refreshed in seconds. Distances would be calculated between Intermediate Computers, which would often be in the middle of the area served, and the Central Computer. Rough calculations for any country around the world show that the system would be updated in less than 15 seconds.

The Intermediate Computers would retrieve information from the servers in their local area and communicate it to the Central Computer, which would itself send updated information to the Intermediate Computers, which would send information to the local servers.

The Intermediate Computers would not upload information from the servers while this process is underway. If payments are made during these 15 seconds, the server would register the payment and our new balance. As the system is so fast, this is of negligible importance.

<u>Calculations for the United States:</u> With an area of 9.6 million square km, we would need 100 Intermediate Computers placed no further than 8,893 km apart. The Central Computer would be located in the middle of the country.

Suppose the average distance between the Central Computer and the Intermediate Computers was 3,500 km. There are 2 different types of connection. The first is between the Central Computer and the Intermediate Computer in order to retrieve data, while the second is the transmission of the updated data on the Central Computer to the Intermediate Computer.

This would involve a distance of 2 x 3,500 km= 7,000 km. As there would be 100 Intermediate Computers, the total distance covered would be 700,000 km. As fiber optics can transmit information at 200,000 km/s, the time required would be 3.5 seconds.

Every Intermediate Computer would have to be in contact with around 2,000 servers located an average of 150 km away. This would cover a distance of 300,000 km, and as 2 connections would be required, the total would be 600,000 km, with the time required to transmit information 3 seconds.

In light of these calculations, refreshing the US system would take 6.5 seconds, with little data being entered into the Central Computer during this time, meaning it would take mere hundredths of a second to perform calculations and to refresh our website.

Although these figures are approximate, they do however demonstrate how quickly information could be transmitted.

Calculations for Spain and countries of a similar size and with a similar population: Here we would use blocks 100 kilometers long, requiring 50 Intermediate Computers, and an average of 400 km between the Central Computer and the Intermediate Computers.

As there are 2 connections, 800 km multiplied by 50 is 40,000 km. As fiber optics can transmit data at a speed of 200,000 km/s, the time required would be 0.20 seconds.

Every block would have approximately 200 servers at an average 50 kilometers apart, meaning a total of 10,000 kilometers would be covered. As there would be 2 connections between the servers and the Intermediate Computers, the total would be 20,000 km. If we divide 20,000 by 200,000, the time required would be 0.1 seconds, which, when added to 0.20, gives us 0.21 seconds to refresh the system.

Given the cost of highways, high-speed trains, and airports, etc., our system would be extremely affordable by comparison.

We would, however, have to prevent vandalism of the fiber-optic system, introducing a law imprisoning anyone perpetrating such a crime for many years.

If the fiber-optic system were down, it would be repaired as soon as possible, with the affected servers accumulating information without downloading it.

Section II.9. Fingerprints

Fingerprints would be registered by means of the index finger and at a resolution of 10,000 x 10,000 bits, although this could be decreased or increased accordingly. There would be international agreements in place in order to set the same resolution for all countries adopting our system.

The system would use the values of 0 and 1, with 0 for no match and 1 for a match. The system would attempt to match a subject with the fingerprints in the database, with our system server performing this operation extremely quickly.

Payment machines would record our fingerprint just like the technology used for individual ID cards.

A kind of digital photo, all you would have to do is place your finger on the payment machine sensor and it would record your fingerprint. Upon removing our finger, the machine would print the receipt in a matter of seconds.

All of our fingers are wider at one point. The payment machine would select the widest line of our index fingerprint, which is where the value would be closest to 1(for a match), located by searching perpendicular to this square matrix with a resolution of 10,000 x 10,000 bits.

The fingerprint to be compared would also have a wider section, which is the first thing to be analyzed by our system server

The server would be able to identify the widest part of the fingerprints in the database, with this saved as standing data in order to make the process as efficient as possible. This would be automatically calculated by payment machines, in order to save our system servers time.

Once the server were to receive the fingerprint data, it would analyze part of the widest horizontal area, comparing the fingerprint received with those in its database. If the horizontal section does not match any in the database, the server would move on to the next fingerprint. In case of a 90% match, the machine would scan the next line immediately above, and if this matches, then the next line above, until it has scanned all of the lines and confirmed the match, with at least a 90% match required for each line.

This process would be extremely fast because if less than 5 dots out of the first 10 were found to match, the system would move to the next fingerprint, meaning it would not have to examine the entire 10,000 dots in the widest part of the fingerprint. If only 2 out of 5 coincided, for example, it would discard the fingerprint and move on to the next one.

Section II.10. Empty bank accounts

If we begin the day with no money in our bank account, or have even gone into our overdraft, or if the Central Computer refreshes the system and the same thing occurs, from that moment on we would only be able to use our credit card to make payments and would only be able to spend money in businesses selling food items, such as bars and restaurants.

Heavy fines would be applied to anyone whose debt exceeded €1,000. Children would be informed that their card had no money left on it, with their guardian responsible for the debt.

One solution for anyone who has run out of money would be to transfer money from another one of their accounts to the account linked to their fingerprint. As the system refresh is almost instant, we would also be able to receive money almost instantaneously.

The bank would automatically upload the transfer to a server in our system. This would be performed by placing the bank server in contact with any of those in our system, which is more convenient than having the Central Computer search for transfers in the bank servers. Nowadays, the Treasury legally searches for evidence of tax fraud in bank servers.

We could also ask a friend to lend us €50 by means of transferring this amount to our account, returning this another day by means of another transfer, which could be performed by cell phone with internet access.

Section II.11. The Central Computer and transfers

Some transfers involve a specific code. When a company wants to charge a payment by means of bank transfer, the server would automatically provide it with a code to be given to the customer. We would need to know the company's corporate tax ID. The Central Computer would register the code both for the entity making the payment and the entity charging it. The invoice would be issued by means of a button on the payment machine, and would then be pending payment.

We have already discussed how this process would be used for sending goods by transport contracted from a third party. We would not have to keep the invoice because the Central Computer would have a record of it, including the code for making the payment, which could also be consulted on our website.

It would be a crime to claim an expense made to a company using its corporate tax ID, if we hadn't actually ordered any goods from said company.

The company targeted would report the other company, instigating an investigation which would examine any email exchange, with the other company demonstrating what it ordered from the company to have reported it, and the costs involved.

As with cell phones, we would be able to access the corporate tax ID of the company we are selling to just as we would look up their telephone number, with all of our customers' corporate tax numbers at our disposal.

If a company were to query any of the goods on an invoice, this would be rectified by means of the invoice number and passed along to the accounts department within the space of a month, because after a month the Central Computer would automatically charge the amount just like direct debit, or after a longer period if agreed to by both parties. If two invoices were found to have the same number, the system would only charge the payment of the one to have been issued more recently.

The payment of these transfers would be performed by accessing our website on the Central Computer and searching for the invoice to be paid. We would order the payment and the computer would search for the transfer code in order to pay the company, meaning that in this case we would not require any server from the system, with accounting records reconciling the entity making the payment with the entity charging it. Such payments would only be paid by means of the bank for imports and exports.

Transfers without codes would be paid as soon as the system is refreshed.

There would also be another system whereby we would provide our international individual ID number, with the company charging us locating this number in the server. Once the payment has been charged, the company would send us our goods. We would send the company our international ID number by means of email.

This system would compete with credit cards and PayPal, with an added advantage the lack of fees associated for purchases less than €100, unlike the systems cited. For purchases over €100, the fees would also be lower. It would also make a company's items cheaper for us.

This system would also be used for electricity bills, car insurance, land value tax, and maintenance fees, etc. These direct payments could be made just as they are now, with companies directly charging our account. In such cases, a company's corporate tax ID would be used instead of the individual ID number.

In both cases, we would provide our data and state that the transaction involves direct debit. In direct debit payments, the bank's server would connect with any one of the servers, transmitting the information to the Central Computer.

Transfers made online would be performed by means of an automatic connection between the bank server and a system server.

Section II.12. Situations which may result in system delays and solutions

The system for the United States or any other country with over 90 million inhabitants would involve anyone away from home entering the state they reside in, with the payment machine selecting the state and thus saving our system servers time.

The logical solution would be for people to be honest when declaring the state they live in. People could pay in other states with any kind of payment method to make this transaction faster.

Without such information, the server would first conduct a search in the current state. If the person's data did not appear, they would then search through the rest of the states, beginning with those closest to the current location, using the same server, and if not found, the person would be identified as an illegal immigrant.

All of the servers across the United States would have a record of all of the digital fingerprints belonging to citizens over the age of 18, in order to avoid the need to access the fingerprint database stored in another state server.

The current servers have 4 microprocessors and can serve 1,000 people at once. There are two types: one which performs tasks and the other which stores websites.

We would use the two types, as one task would be to search for fingerprints and we would need very few servers storing our websites.

A regular computer can perform almost 1,000 million operations per second by means of a single microprocessor. The combination of 4 microprocessors could perform well over 4,000 million operations, as it would use microprocessors that are much faster than a regular computer.

In a city of 200,000 people, less than 1,000 would be making purchases at the same time, with this figure perhaps being closer to 40. If a 41st person initiated a purchase, the system would divert to another server, as analyzing 40 fingerprints at once would be faster than 1,000. For countries with a population of 40 to 50 million, searches would be instant if we used the 40 people option.

Other countries with a greater population would use groups less than 40 to ensure the searches would be fast and cost efficient. Both minor cards and company cards would not require fingerprint analysis, making payments faster.

We would use our own servers as all the fingerprints would occupy a lot of memory. In countries with over 60 million inhabitants, we would have to increase the capacity of our existing servers, as these hold 8,000 GB. All of this would, however, depend on the fingerprint resolution.

We might suppose that with 10,000 servers for the performing of tasks, we could cover an entire country with a population of 40 to 50 million, because in a city of 200,000 people, 10 servers would be enough, because 400 people would hardly all attempt to pay for a product at the same time. Small towns would however require at least 1 or 2 servers.

Servers more powerful than those currently available could be developed in order to produce results in fractions of a second, meaning more than 40 people could make transactions at the same time, using more microprocessors.

Large computers would be made by using multiple microprocessors. This more expensive option would make searching for fingerprints in China, the United States, and India an instant process, without the need for the payment machine to select the customer's home state.

A financial study would be required into the viability; as such countries would require many servers. I don't believe it would be worth it in countries such as Mexico or Brazil.

For foreigners in countries in which our system has not been implemented, it would be easier to pay by card. This would be better for both parties because it would save both our time and that of the company we are making the payment to. An example of this would be a Chinese man purchasing an item in Russia.

Studying the world's fiber-optic maps reveals a substantial network.

Telecommunications engineers would have to perform exact calculations for every country around the world, although this process would be quite straightforward, as demonstrated by the approximate calculations provided here.

CHAPTER III

The sophisticated system

Section III.1. Description and advantages

The sophisticated system involves uploading to a server all of the items on a supplier's invoice, as well as a detailed list of all our expenses; such as in a supermarket.

The manufacture of explosives, chemical weapons, and illegal arms could also be investigated, as could consumption, serving as a great advantage.

Section III.2. Municipal Computers

The use of a single Central Computer would be too slow due to the sheer volume of information sent to it over the fiber-optic network.

Whenever goods or a service are purchased in a store, the payment machine would send basic information to the Central Computer servers, such as the purchase made and the date, etc. The same server would also send information on the items purchased.

Every municipality would have its own computer, with large cities having various computers organized according to area.

Data could be transferred to another area or a different municipality by means of the postal code.

Municipal Computers would not be as powerful as the Central Computer, as they would operate with much less data. They would also store data on companies and individuals registered as residents in a particular municipality. They would also retrieve information for anyone changing banks, which would be useful for searching items.

Changing banks from the one in which our fingerprint is registered would automatically deactivate the credit cards in our former bank.

As stated in the previous chapter, supplier invoices would be both printed and registered on their payment machine. The person making the purchase would enter their card and the payment machine would upload the total amount owed to a server in the Central Computer, with the items on the invoice uploaded to the same server as in our system. Items on invoices to be charged would also be uploaded with codes.

The server used by the Central Computer would locate the fingerprint and register it, with the same server used for the Municipal Computer so that it wouldn't have to search for the fingerprint again, instead using the entry already found, registering all of the items.

The Municipal Computer would register items on the invoices in its servers. It would also register items purchased as expenses by employee credit cards, in order to better monitor such purchases.

The Municipal Computer would have a record of items purchased as expenses, income, and the total balance.

Refreshing the Municipal Computer would also be extremely fast, as hardly any data is involved.

With regard to the search for explosives and chemical weapons, these could be bought by factories and chemistry departments, etc. Individual chemists would not be able to purchase them, nor would they be able to buy material to set up a laboratory, with laboratories requiring legal permits. This would make the search much more efficient.

Municipal Computers would have to review the last 3 years of data registered, as people could buy one chemical substance one day and a different one a day later, using the combination to manufacture explosives or chemical weapons. Such individuals could also move to another municipality during these 3 years, obligating them to contact the computer in the municipality moved to.

A maximum upper threshold would be set for food purchases made by fingerprint, with this figure around €500 per person per month in Spain, without taking into account individual lunches or dinners consumed in restaurants. In other countries this figure would be different. If the amount spent exceeded €500 per person in a single family, the Municipal Computer would advise the Central Computer, opening an investigation into slave labor. Fluctuations would also be analyzed, such as consumption jumping from €150 to €350.

Inspectors from the Department of Labor would check if slaves were being forced to work and eat in the same restaurant.

All of these minimum rates for expenditure would be evaluated depending on the number of children and whether children out of employment were living with parents, etc. The Municipal Computer would conduct such an evaluation by means of the Municipal Registry and the Department of Labor.

Section III.3. System operations within a single country and duplicate data

Anyone from Chicago making purchases in New York would require the New York server to download information on them from the Chicago server for their local municipality.

The Chicago server for their local area would then update the information in seconds, meaning that they would be able to consult their spending in detail with a simple cell phone with internet access by consulting the website for their local municipality or, in this case, the area of the city they live in.

Future investigations by the Treasury would be able to browse detailed information on incoming payments on the New York server, in order for the computer for the particular area of the city to record the items a company sells, however this would also be registered in the Chicago server, so that individuals could be investigated (in case they keep slaves or manufacture arms, etc.), meaning data for items purchased would be duplicated.

Section III.4. Our programs and those used by the system

With this system, companies would not need to use specific programs, as the Municipal Computer would update company stock, even analyzing anything missing.

Individuals or companies would only have to consult their website on the Central Computer to check their accounts and access the municipal website to check information on particular items.

Section III.5. False invoices and receipts

An individual could request for an invoice or a receipt to be fudged by changing the items on it, with the best strategy only having a single item on it.

This would be useful for men visiting strip clubs, meaning that the information uploaded online would be false. In this case, for example, the Municipal Computer would know the items purchased, but the strip club would appear on the receipt as though it were a restaurant.

Receipts fudged on our personal websites would allow men to hide detailed information on their spending from their wives, or for women to hide information on their expenditure on jewels and in hair salons, etc. This would be useful if there is little trust between us and the people we share our life with.

The most useful example would be with gifts, allowing us to surprise people. In such cases, the different items on the receipt would be registered on our website as 'gifts'.

This would also be useful for monitoring teenagers' spending if they are not to be trusted, as they wouldn't be able to hide purchases made.

Freelancers and companies would not be able to hide items on invoices.

Section III.6. The system in the European Union

If our system were to be adopted by the entire European Union, items purchased could be uploaded to a server in our municipality from another country, such as France, for example. This server would then communicate with any of the national servers, which would have data stored on our municipality of residence, uploading the information to the relevant computer in our municipality. The items purchased in France would be translated to our local language by our Municipal Computer.

While in France, we would be able to consult our spending by means of a simple cell phone with internet access, accessing the website for our local municipality.

This example is very similar to that previously given for New York and Chicago.

Section III.7. How to prevent fraud

In order to prevent fraud, every council would provide 2 people from the parties to hold a majority with a 128-gigabyte optical pencil holding information on all of the transactions to have been made the previous day in the municipality, or in areas of large cities. For such cities, one optical pencil would be designated to each area.

To prevent invoices being erased from Municipal Computers, the Central Computer would check all invoices for all municipalities at set intervals, verifying the total value on the invoice and the date.

In order to prevent fraud on the Central Computer, all Municipal Computers would perform a check once a month on the total value and the dates on the invoices in the Central Computer, to ensure the head of the Central Computer is behaving in an honest manner. Such cross-checking would make fraud almost impossible.

In cases of suspected fraud, the representatives of the political parties would be informed by means of their optical pencils.

Section III.8. The 100% sophisticated system

In order to ensure that the system is 100 percent sophisticated, we would have to take into account spending made on debit and credit cards, as well as via PayPal. We would only use these cards when we don't have any money, when using the internet, or when on vacation abroad

Our bank book would show our total expenditure, however the bank would also know all of the establishments in which we had spent our money.

The bank would have to automatically upload all items bought from a business using our card to a server in our municipality, meaning these card payment systems would have to be changed.

Foreigners on vacation use their credit cards to make purchases, however we are unable to update a store's stock because the current system doesn't show the different items purchased. Such foreigners wouldn't be able to make more purchases once the time they are legally allowed to spend in a country has expired, as the courts would cancel their card. Payment machines would know if foreigners were using different cards than the one registered at border control, because the card number would be uploaded to the servers. The card payment machine would communicate with the server checking the validity of the card. It could also be designed in order that we would be informed if the person was wanted by police.

Even in our country of residence, we may also find ourselves in a supermarket without any money and wish to use our credit card. We might also buy items that are not food items, meaning the current system is unable to inform us how much a family really spends on food.

When making these payments, therefore, the business charging the payment would upload the total and all of the items to the card center as well as to a server in the municipality in which the business is located, as well as to the municipality of the person paying, meaning the municipality would be able to identify the buyer if the person's or company's postal code were added to the card information.

For cards used by foreigners on vacation, this would not be necessary as they would not keep slaves. They would, however, be prohibited from buying any item that could be used to manufacture arms or explosives.

When we use the internet, card centers would upload the items to the respective municipalities. If these payments are to countries in which our system has not been adopted, the items would only be uploaded to our municipality. Cards used online would show which country they were from.

Section III.9. Stolen and destroyed goods and how to prevent fraud

This sophisticated system would have to account for stolen goods, products to become obsolete or to have expired, and those to be destroyed.

We would update stolen or destroyed stock by accessing the municipal website, with the Municipal Computer checking that such corrections were plausible. The Municipal Computer would also automatically update stock totals as items are sold.

Drugs might be sold as follows: if a clothes shop sales were low, it could sell drugs and destroy the clothes. A drug addict could spend €2,000 a month on drugs in a year.

The Municipal Computer would have to check the purchases made from the business; therefore a tax inspector would be sent out to customers' homes to verify if they did indeed have the quantity of clothes purchased.

This practice could be extended to any type of business, as nobody spends €4,000 every month in the same coffee shop, for example. Such a sum could be spent in a jeweler's, however. The Municipal Computer would have data on every individual's purchasing power.

Section III.10. Imports and exports

There would be no problem in the European Union as long as our system was adopted by all of the countries in the community.

When a company exports goods, a detailed invoice would be uploaded to the municipal server in the country to which the goods were being sent, along with the invoice total. The server would assign a code in order that we could be paid by means of a bank transfer. The items sold would also be uploaded to our municipal server, in order to reflect stock totals.

The opposite process would be used for imports, whereby the company selling to us would upload the invoice, with this communicated to our national Central Computer, with the total value and all of the items communicated to the Municipal Computer along with a code generated by the Municipal Server in the other country, allowing us to make the transfer. The other country would upload the items to the server in their municipality in order to update stock totals. This would be the same for transfers with codes.

In both cases the information would not be reconciled with accounts, as those of the other country are not of interest to us.

Imports or exports to countries that do not use our system would be more complex, as customs would be involved, charging the relevant tariffs.

In these cases, goods would come attached with a paper invoice, with the customs in a country uploading the information to the servers by means of the company tax ID, and both detailed and simplified versions of the invoice.

In the case of exports, customs would upload all items to the servers in our municipality, with payment pending by means of a code generated by customs.

In countries in which our system has not been adopted, we would be paid by means of a bank transfer to our company account with the code added for reference.

When the bank transfer arrives in our account, it would automatically upload the total value and the reference code to one of the servers.

Upon refresh, the information would be transferred to the Central Computer and added to the company accounts. The total would be checked and the code added to the company accounts. Only bank transfers with codes would be permitted.

If the invoice is incorrect, the Central Computer would send an automatic email to the bank in order that the amount is returned, advising the company with an automatic email in order that it can contact the foreign company by means of email, communicating that the invoice is incorrect and that the correct invoice must be sent in due course. This process would continue until the correct invoice has been sent.

If we were to import goods, customs would upload the items to servers in our municipality, along with the total, which we would pay by means of a bank transfer featuring a code generated by customs.

Customs would receive an email from the foreign company communicating that the payment had been made, with customs then updating a server with this information, in order that the next system refresh would transmit this information to the Central Computer, changing the relevant record in our accounts.

Section III.11. The consultations and their technology

If we have internet at home or on our cell phone then this would be straightforward. We would be able to consult the various items uploaded to our Municipal Computer within a given time period.

Children and teenagers would be able to consult their transactions by means of their card number, as they would also have a website.

Anyone without a home internet connection, or anyone unable to use the internet, would ask the bank for a paper copy of their monthly expenditure, paying the bank a fee for this service.

Our bank passbooks would be updated once a week to show our expenditure, although detailed information would not be provided. The Municipal Computer would store information on bank accounts and would download information on our incoming and outgoing payments every night from the bank linked to our fingerprint, regardless of the payment method.

We would pay our bank a minimal fee for a list of all the items purchased in a week, with this information produced in paper format.

With this extra information, banks would have to increase the amount of memory available on their servers or increase the number of servers.

We would not need to connect to the Central Computer in order to consult information stored on it, as previously mentioned. We would instead use web storage servers, which would be updated every time the system is refreshed. Information would be stored on the last 5 years; however the Central Computer would store all our information until our death. After 5 years, the servers would erase the information. In order to access information from before this period, we would use a password to access the Central Computer, with the only drawback being that the process would take longer.

The servers would be located a short distance from the Central Computer, in order that the system may be refreshed immediately.

To consult detailed information on income and expenditure, we would use the servers closest to our Municipal Computer. This would work in the same way as described for the Central Computer.

CHAPTER IV

The bunker

The bunker would house the Central Computer and the various banks, with cash held in the departments corresponding to each bank. The national bank would also be housed in the bunker, as this would facilitate lending to other banks, performed by means of cash transfers via machines kept in the bunker.

When different banks are involved in incoming and outgoing payments, at the end of the day each bank would find itself with either a deficit or a surplus of our money and the money it uses for investments.

Due to this, once a day the Central Computer would run a program to gauge how much cash has been transferred into or out of every bank department.

We have already explained how this money is moved around.

The process wouldn't be used if the bank were national; however the European Union prohibits monopolies. It could be national in other countries.

The bank would have its own money accumulated from its own businesses and commissions, with this separate.

The entire online system for foreign payments would remain the same.

The main advantage of our system for transferring cash is that it would prevent financial black holes, like what happened with the Lehman Brothers and with soccer teams, etc. Bookkeeping would be performed on a daily basis by means of corporate and individual withholdings.

Cash does, of course, need to be moved around, because when Greece was rescued cash was sent to the banks.

Inspections of companies, individuals, banks, unions, and foundations would be more efficient because of the many inspectors in the bunker. If an invoice were to be flagged as suspicious, the inspectors would communicate this to the computer in the corresponding municipality, examining the items.

The bunker would be sound in construction and earthquake proof. It would be built underground and in the middle of the country, in order to facilitate communication with the Intermediate Computers, and far from any city.

The bunker would be protected by the military, as there would be a landing strip for the arrival of airplanes carrying cash, in case an international bank ran out of money.

The bunker would also be fitted with a missile shield like that in New York, in order to protect it from bombs. Commercial airplanes would be allowed to fly overhead but military airplanes would not, even if national.

To enable satellite communications, aerials would have to be installed, with care taken to prevent vandalism.

Satellite connections would be used to investigate Latvian computers from Spain, for example, with fiber optics used for short distances.

3 shifts would be established, as the system would run continually, with constant monitoring in place in case a computer breaks down and requires replacing.

CHAPTER V

The economy

Section V.1. The system, its investigative activities, and automatic tax declarations

Bookkeeping for companies and individuals would be automatic, with minimal effort required on our part.

The only details needed by the system would the total on an invoice, the accounting record, the VAT (or the relevant taxes used by countries outside the European Union), and any deductible expenses, as the standard chart of accounts encompasses sales, purchases, and repayments, etc.

The Central Computer would have two accounting programs: one for our company bookkeeping and the other for our personal tax declaration.

All of our related payments would be handled by the Central Computer, rather than the Municipal Computer.

Repayments would be made by the Central Computer, providing the company information on our repayment schedule, with the company able to access the data in the Central Computer. The company website would then be updated if the Central Computer detects fluctuations upon refreshing the system.

We mentioned that advisory firms would not have as much work, however one of their roles would be to devise salaries according to overtime worked and commission, etc. This information would be sent to the Central Computer in order to register payments to different employees.

Nowadays in Spain, invoices of €3,000 from the same supplier are cross checked. Our system would cross check all invoices and receipts, except for those reflecting items purchased by foreigners not registered in our national fingerprint system, nor in the European Union. Spending by minors would also not be checked, as they would not complete tax declarations.

Such investigations may seem unnecessary, however they would be performed for security reasons, as invoices for sales or purchases could be removed from the online system, particularly by corrupt politicians.

By cross checking such invoices and flagging errors, the Municipal Computer would investigate the matter, or the computer for the local area in a large city.

It would be unusual for two companies to agree to erase both a sale and a purchase from the system, as wiping the invoice would benefit the purchaser but not the seller.

Upon detecting fraud, the Municipal Computer would be rectified, or those for the two municipalities if the buyer and seller belong to two different municipalities or areas of a large city. The total on the Central Computer would also have to be corrected or erased, which would be almost impossible, requiring a report and an investigation by means of the politicians' optical pencils.

As cash would not be used and banks would be monitored, corruption would plummet.

Nowadays, investigations are made into multiple current accounts belonging to companies and individuals. Our system is superior because only one account would be consulted, meaning that if we allow for tax havens, the money sent to such accounts would be legalized, which would render them pointless, as their very existence emerged to facilitate tax fraud.

Profits made by companies are shared in different ways among the partners. The Central Computer would record information on how profits are shared, however the servers would not. Notary publics would enter the data directly into the Central Computer whenever companies are founded or changes are made. Such information would also be used for automatic personal income tax declarations after profits have been shared between the partners. Information on the profits shared would be transmitted to the Central Computer, with any remainder producing tax benefits.

Expenditure on personal tax declarations may be deductible, such as the purchase of a new car. The money spent on these deductible expenses would be returned to us by the Treasury from money it withholds each day. Such returns would be automatically generated once a year, as though the Treasury is refunding our money. What we pay each year to the Treasury would be subtracted from our account for income and expenditure, both for companies and individuals.

Apart from slave labor, which would be punished by imprisonment, there are another two forms of tax fraud.

The first kind of fraud is that of social security, with this consisting of working more hours than those stipulated and earning the same salary, such as being hired to work 4 hours and actually working 8. In this case, the employee would receive social security benefits corresponding to the 4-hour work day contract, completing 2 hours of social work. This kind of fraud could be prevented by prohibiting part-time contracts.

The second form of fraud would be that of working for a family member who does not pay your social security contributions, paying your salary by means of legal bank transfers.

This kind of fraud would be preventable, because anyone who does not declare themselves rich would have to seek employment and complete social work in order to make social security contributions. Studying and providing some assistance to the family member would however be permitted, rendering social security fraud minimal

Combating these kinds of fraud would involve increasing the number of inspectors from the Department of Labor.

All of a country's financial movements would be registered, demonstrating that there would be practically no tax fraud, underground economies, or black money, as banks, freelancers, small and medium-sized companies, multinationals, unions, foundations, and politicians, etc., would be closely monitored.

Section V.2. Companies' maximum and minimum profit thresholds

If a supplier were to sell us a carton of juice for €0.60, we would not be able to re-sell it for €40, because the Central Computer would think we'd sold our customer juice with a side of drugs.

It would be convenient if fines for surpassing the maximum profit threshold were extremely heavy, in order to intimidate people and facilitate investigation into their activities.

It would also be prohibited for political parties to inflate invoices for self-financing purposes.

The maximum profit thresholds would be developed by the Treasury for all types of businesses and professions.

Agreements would be in place between companies of the same type in order to set prices, with a minimum profit threshold set for one type of business, preventing unfair trade, such as establishments selling coffee for €0.60 and others selling it for €1.20.

Section V.3. Businesses and debt

Debt would be tolerated; however a period would be given for its repayment, such as 30, 60, or 90 days, or another timeframe agreed upon by both parties. Upon the period elapsing, the Central Computer would become responsible for charging the payment. All of the measures previously mentioned are intended to ensure that companies would always get paid, which is why transfers would be performed with a code, for example.

Payments could only be deferred to the next year, and not any longer.

If a company did not have the money to pay its bills, the Central Computer would send an automatically-generated email advising it to take out a loan or organize a capital injection by one of the partners, etc. The company's non-compliance would see its assets seized, meaning there would be no need for debt collectors.

Soccer clubs with astronomical debts would also be a thing of the past, as would council debts with their suppliers.

No company would be able to remain in business with debt, and would be dissolved. Councils currently receive funding from the state, which issues public debt in order to redress the deficit, or else has to be rescued, like Greece. Under our system, it would not be necessary to issue debts as there would be no deficit.

For the entire computer system to work properly, money would be needed to pay for things.

Public limited companies issue shares, while private limited companies increase their capital. All of this would be notarized by a notary public, who would inform the Central Computer of such injections, including them in the company accounts.

Section V.4. Modules

Payments of fixed quantities to the Treasury (known as "modules") would not exist, as it would be ridiculous to use this system when we have detailed information for different businesses at our disposal.

Section V.5. Deductible items and VAT

In order to perform bookkeeping, the Central Computer would have to know which items are deductible. This would be similar to the current system, as though the Treasury were to carry out an inspection and we were to submit all of our receipts for deductible expenses. The servers would then deduct the value of the items and this information would be communicated to the Central Computer.

Coffee purchased in coffee shops would not constitute deductible expenses, instead serving as income for these coffee shops, unless purchased by politicians, of course.

The system would only need to know the payment method. If a payment were made using a fingerprint or with a card that does not belong to a particular company, the system would believe this to be a non-deductible expense, whereas if a company card or that belonging to a freelancer were used, the system would know if the item were deductible or not.

The different purchases would also have item codes stating if they were deductible or not. This could be performed as follows: the server would have a list of all deductible expenses such as lentils or shampoo, without the need to include brands. Books would be classified, such as chemistry books, poetry books, or cookery books, etc.

If I were to use my company card to buy shampoo, this would only be deductible if I owned or worked at a hair salon. If I didn't work at a hair salon, a dispute would break out between my boss and me once they discovered the expense.

Every company would be able to investigate its own spending on its municipal website, which would show a list of the deductible items forwarded to the Central Computer. This would allow companies to investigate their own employees, as they would be informed of all payments made using their cards.

If we were to pay for a meal with our company card, for example, this would be a deductible expense, such as when an employee uses transport for one reason or another.

Regular employees would not be able to use company bank cards on weekends, because they might use them for vacation or weekend spending. In order not to over-complicate the system, it would interpret any weekend expenditure as non-deductible, despite the fact that an employee could indeed be working over the period, with a dispute breaking out between the boss and the employee upon the former discovering that the latter was not, indeed, working on a Saturday or Sunday.

If we did, indeed, want to complicate the system, the company would have to inform the Central Computer of employee vacation periods, in order for the company card to be deactivated during this time, with the card activated on weekends for employees who work on these days.

The server would be able to apply VAT thanks to codes for the different businesses we would spend our money in, with this VAT paid once the product has been charged. In countries with other taxes, the same system would also apply.

Section V.6. Reserve funds and politicians' allowances

In our computer system, funds would be set aside for exclusive use by the Council of Ministers, the head of the computer system, and a series of trusted inspectors.

These reserve funds would be used for tackling terrorism and paying police informers and spies, etc.

The spending of these funds would be registered with cards, similar to the employee spending scheme but used among police officers and spies, etc. The funds would be factored into the general national budgets as special expenses. The system head would be able to investigate such spending, to prevent anyone from illegally stealing the funds.

Special fingerprint machines would be used to pay police informers, with the amount able to exceed €50. This code would allow the Central Computer to waive transfers over €50 to people who are not family members of the relevant police officer or spy, etc.

It would be preferable if politicians did not receive allowances, as these could confuse our computer system by appearing as non-deductible expenses.

Politicians could instead receive a fixed sum each year, with research required to decide whether such a sum should be subject to taxation.

This would allow politicians to purchase shoes, suits, gifts for their wives, and coffee, as well as to pay fines, just as they do now.

Another possibility would be for the expenses to be deductible, reverted back into the council or another body.

To give an example, when all of a city's councilmen want to buy suits, such expenses could be deducted upon the presentation of a receipt from a clothing store; however a single councilman would not be allowed to buy 5 suits on council expenses with the card given to him.

Our computer system could also be configured so that such allowances could only be spent on hotels, restaurants, trains, buses, and airplanes, as long as the travel was accounted for.

Tax inspectors could be designated to cover each of a country's provinces and provided with data on all politicians' cards in order to track their spending.

Section V.7. When is bookkeeping performed?

Bookkeeping would be performed at 5 o' clock in the morning, as fluctuations would occur during the day thanks to returns and corrections. The process would be almost instantaneous thanks to the speed of the Central Computer.

Due to the withholdings made, the calculations would be partial, with official bookkeeping performed on an annual basis.

All cash transfers in the bunker would commence at 6 a.m., once the Central Computer has performed its bookkeeping and the program has indicated that money has been automatically transferred.

Any calculations performed by the Central Computer would include a date and time given down to the second. If we were to run the program at 5 a.m., for example, it would inform us of all the data produced over the last 24 hours. If I were to make a purchase at 05:01, for example, this would be included in the following day's accounts.

Section V.8. Personal Income Tax

If we all made a living from a single income, tax would be straightforward. Things get complicated, however, when people start earning money from the stock market and renting out apartments. As long as data is provided to the Treasury's computers, nowadays all of this can be very efficiently tracked.

The main advantage with our computer system over the current system is that data would not have to be entered manually.

Nowadays many people file their tax declarations online, meaning employees do not enter their own data.

To make the system more secure, however, the Central Computer would track all movements.

If we were to sign a rental contract, for example, the Central Computer would have to be informed. A contract would be necessary because rent normally exceeds €300 per month and landlords are not normally family members. This book would be extremely long if we were to go into such details, as the system has many facets. This book merely sets the foundations for the future.

Section V.9. The national bank, the Public Treasury, and the councils.

The Public Treasury would also have a single bank account in the Central Computer, with all revenue generated channeled into the national bank.

In drawing up the state budgets, electronic money would be distributed among all of the institutions (such as councils, unions, and foundations, etc.).

All institutions would operate with electronic money, just like any other company, and would therefore have a single account for their income and expenditure.

If the various institutions were operating with a deficit, the state would redress the balance. Our system would not be applicable to any country operating with a deficit despite eliminating tax fraud.

Transfers could be made between all of the various institutions, with the Central Computer interpreting these transfers as though between NGOs. Transfers would also be permitted between institutions and professionals, in line with the laws on minimum and maximum profit thresholds.

Section V.10. Under our system, everyone would get paid

All those unemployed would receive benefits. This is currently only in effect in Alaska, where the unemployed receive $2,500 per year, however it could be implemented in at least 30 countries, whereby dismissals would be free and companies would therefore run more efficiently.

Some countries, such as Switzerland, would be against such a policy.

Foreigners would not be eligible for unemployment benefits.

One advantage of unemployment benefits is that they stimulate consumption, which is another problem in many capitalist countries currently mired in recession.

Under our system, everyone would be eligible except the rich, married couples in which one partner works, and students, with everyone else searching for a job when they reach the eligible age.

Close monitoring would be in effect. Anyone out of work would be paid for social work undertaken over a period of hours, such as looking after elderly people in poverty, and would spend the rest of their time on the job hunt.

As there will always be some people who are neither rich nor inclined to work, a vagrancy act would be implemented, imprisoning such people if they turn down at least 6 jobs in their profession over a period of 2 years. They would be safer in prison, because otherwise they could become dangerous criminals.

With such extensive unemployment protection, there is a possibility that people might generate conflict at work in order to be dismissed, with anyone who is repeatedly dismissed subject to investigation, and their unemployment benefits gradually reduced until their behavior improves.

The distribution of unemployment benefits would increase public spending; however such spending would be reduced by lowering the number of staff working at the Internal Revenue and other bodies such as the police. Savings could also be made on electricity, security staff, cleaning, and buildings.

In less capitalist countries, begging may be authorized, which could be performed by means of a transfer of €0.20 or another quantity that does not exceed €50 per day, €300 per month or €3,600 per year, with the poor person in question handing over the details of the bank account linked to their fingerprint. In such cases, transfers would be performed by means of satellite with a simple cell phone with internet access.

Section V.11. How to eliminate debt, using Spain as an example

The following formula would be valid for many countries. In the European Union, it would be most successful in Italy, where money lost to tax fraud accounts for 27% of the national GDP. In Spain, this figure is 25%, although Europe's powerhouse, Germany, also has a particularly high figure at 16% of the GDP. Practically all of this tax fraud could be eliminated, as we have explained.

In Spain, the GDP is approximately €1 billion, meaning fraud is worth some €250,000 million.

We would drastically lower taxes in order to attract companies, as then more taxes would be paid. Despite the lack of serious research into tax fraud, many sources suggest it ranges from €200,000 to €250,000 million. The lowest figure I've heard used is €160,000 million.

These dramatic tax cuts would allow us to reduce the figure of €250,000 million per year to €150,000 million.

We could use €80,000 million of this €150,000 million to pay off Spain's public debt over a 13-year period.

13 years is just an example, as it could take longer if we don't implement the book's computer system as soon as possible, because the debt is forecast to exceed 100% in coming years. It may not even take as long as 13 years, if, instead of the average €9,000 per year handed out in unemployment benefits in Spain, serious research was conducted proving a lower sum to be viable. Or if this amount were to be even higher, then it would take longer.

€30,000 million is currently being paid out to the unemployed. We would increase this to 50,000 million for anyone not earning a single salary, and to people working part time.

These figures are approximate, as the national GDP is calculated by the Bank of Spain and may not be exact. Unemployment benefits would also be raised thanks to the redundancies produced by our streamlining of the civil service.

€100,000 million of the €150,000 million would thus be channeled into spending; leaving a surplus of €50,000 million that would pay off the current deficit.

€9,000 would be an average figure, as someone who is out of work at the age of 25 would receive less, for example. All of this would need to be meticulously calculated, with the figures quoted here mere examples, and these calculations performed under consideration of social questions. Another example would be a married couple without children who are both unemployed, with only one of them to receive benefits, etc.

After the 13 years, we would no longer have to direct €80,000 million toward eliminating public debt, as it would have been wiped, therefore this money could be channeled into social projects.

We would have to add the €38,000 million that we are currently paying in interest on the debt, which would no longer exist upon the elimination of the debt, which would be another 3.8%. This €38,000 million would gradually decrease over the 13 years, although interest rates may rise.

With that said, I do not believe that such a system would jeopardize pension funds, as over the 13 years, money from tax fraud would be paid into pensions, which would increase according to annual inflation, instead of social security taking care of them.

Social security could also be lowered, as businesses would be more productive and create more jobs as a consequence.

Spain is ranked number 25 in terms of per capita income, and could eliminate its debt by lowering taxes by 30 to 40%.

It would be easier still for other countries:

Germany: With a GDP of €3 billion, 5.2% unemployment, tax fraud accounting for 16% of its GDP and public debt worth 72.5% of its GDP, this debt could also be paid off and taxes lowered. The deficit is also almost zero.

France has a GDP of €2.1 billion, 10.2% unemployment, tax fraud accounting for 15% of its GDP and public debt worth 93.5% of its GDP, which could be paid and taxes lowered.

Japan has a GDP of €5.2 billion and tax fraud accounts for 12% of its GDP; however the public debt is 240%, which could be lowered, but over a longer period of time.

As China's GDP is worth €13 billion and tax fraud accounts for 11%, its public debt worth 6% of the GDP could be paid off very quickly.

The United States has a GDP of €13.2 billion, 6% unemployment, and public debt of 104%, however tax fraud only accounts for 8.6% of its GDP, which could be lowered but not paid off, as the deficit is over 5%. The deficit would have to be lowered; however taxes would must remain high, with corporate tax 32.7%.

The current economic policies used in the countries cited mean public debt is rising and will not be able to be paid off. This has sparked a grave crisis in capitalist countries and a reemergence of communism in Spain, Venezuela, and Greece.

Any country could be studied, with conclusions reached on our system's potential to eradicate its tax fraud.

The calculation involves taking the annual amount lost to tax fraud and using it to pay off the public deficit, which would produce a surplus for almost any country in the world.

CHAPTER VI

How the various businesses would run under our system

Section VI.1. Slot machines

As there would be no coins with which play slot machines, we would have to use our fingerprints.

We would specify the number of games we wished to play by placing our finger on a sensor.

Foreigners would play with credit or debit cards by entering their PIN.

Information on income or expenditure on these machines would not be cross checked for foreigners' accounts.

Cards belonging to minors would not work on slot machines.

The money accumulated in the machines would be divided between the owner of the establishment, the company to which the machines belong, and the Treasury. Internally, the machine would be designed so that it knew how much it owed the each of these recipients, with the information uploaded to a server in our system.

If the user of a slot machine were to win a game, they would collect their winnings by means of placing their finger on a sensor, or if foreign, by entering their credit or debit card.

Machine technicians would only be called out if machines stopped working, or to change programs or a machine itself.

Machines would not accept company or politicians' cards. It would be scandalous for politicians to spend our money on slot machines, as it would for employees to spend company money on such a pursuit.

Section VI.2. Cigarette machines

Cigarette machines would be fitted with fingerprint sensors, with cigarettes available for purchase among those over 18 with sufficient funds in their accounts.

This would be convenient for buyers because they wouldn't have to wait for the machines to be activated, as well as for waiters, saving them time.

Cigarette machines could therefore be installed outdoors.

Minors would not be able to use their cards, nor would politicians, or employees using company cards.

Section VI.3. Vending machines

This time, minors and politicians would be able to use their cards.

All cigarette, slot, and vending machines could also be operated with credit cards, with users entering their PIN, as this would be very useful for foreigners. Company cards could not be used; as such purchases do not constitute company expenses.

Section VI.4. Shows and sporting events

Fingerprints could be used to purchase tickets for cinemas, theaters, soccer games and concerts, etc. Anyone who is a member of a soccer club would also be able to use their membership card to pay for their tickets.

Controversy recently broke out concerning the 21% VAT rate charged on theater tickets, as only 4% VAT is charged on books, and both activities are cultural. VAT is charged the moment the purchase is made.

Section VI.5. Bank commission

Making payments very often involves two different banks, with banks charging us a small commission if the amount transferred is over €100.

When information on the transfer reaches the Central Computer, the Computer would configure the transfer as an incoming payment for the bank to receive our money, and as an outgoing payment from the bank account linked to our fingerprint, just like a regular invoice between banks.

The bank would have its own business and charge commission for the running of its current accounts.

Loans would appear in the accounting system as an injection of money, with the interest charged by the bank appearing as a regular invoice between the bank and its customers.

Banks would be treated just like any other private company, meaning that it would have a single national account for its income and expenditure and would not be allowed to fall into debt. It would however have branches, with each branch given its own website.

Section VI.6. How to sell on our jewelry and stamps, etc.

To sell on our jewelry and stamps, we would go to specialist dealers such as stamp collectors, with special payment machines used in these establishments so that we can be paid into our current account by means of fingerprint sensors.

The same would occur in pawnshops and with art dealers buying art from our homes.

All of these specialists would have special machines that generate codes. Instead of the server, the payment machine would generate a unique code in order for the business to complete its accounts. The code would be the corporate tax number of the business paying us.

Such payments could exceed €50 per day, €300 per month, or €3,600 per year.

Section VI.7. Casinos, unregulated gambling, and betting

Just like under the current system, players at a casino would receive chips by means of payment by fingerprint or credit or debit card.

We would receive money for returned chips in the current account linked to our fingerprint, along with a code which would allow the casino's activities to be monitored.

Cards belonging to minors, politicians, or to employees would not be valid for use in casinos.

Unregulated gambling would be tolerated as long as a person's winnings do not exceed €3,600 per year.

Gambling would be permitted with players using chips and cell phones with internet connections. Winnings would be entered into our account by means of online transfer at the end of the game and with a daily cap of €50.

In order to trick the Central Computer, anyone winning €100 in a single day could ask for the transfer to be divided into two and transferred on two different days, just as winnings of €500 could be divided into 10 transfers of €50 over a two-month period.

Playing dominoes with the loser paying for the winner's coffee would be less problematic, because losers would be able to pay up by means of their fingerprint.

Bets of small quantities would also be allowed between friends as long as they don't exceed €50, with transfers of €20 made to the winner, for example, or other quantities that don't exceed €50. Such transfers would be performed instantly by means of cell phones connected to the internet.

Section VI.8. The lottery, betting on sports, bingo, and horseracing

Lottery winnings and those for other legal forms of gambling would be paid out by means of bank transfer, minus the 20% charged by the Treasury on large amounts, with small winnings paid out by means of fingerprint machines.

Bingo would operate off a similar system, also using fingerprints. Payment for cards would be made by placing our fingerprint on the machine sensor, with company and politicians' cards invalid.

Legal betting establishments, such as those for betting on soccer games, would operate online, just like under the current system. The Central Computer would be informed of all transactions, because payments would be made via PayPal or via credit or debit card.

For horseracing, racecourses would pay out winnings by means of the fingerprint system.

Section VI.9. Collect on delivery

As we would always have to sell things legally, the following would only apply to companies.

Postal workers would enter the data into a computer, asking for our company card and name of the item to be sold.

The postal service would charge us a commission, which would be charged from our company card. The fingerprint system would not be valid for such a payment. The postal service computer system would take the company details and charge the commission, just like under the current system.

Once the product has been received, the recipient would place their finger or the company card on the postal worker's machine. If collect on delivery were not activated, the package would be returned just like under the present system, with the company losing money, as it paid the postal service to send the goods out in the first place. If the customer pays for the items, the postal worker would upload them to a server and record the payment made.

Section VI.10. Soccer transfers

No cash would be required because transfers would be paid by bank transfer. The kind of fraud to have occurred in the past would also be stamped out, such as soccer players with a fee €10 million being allocated one of €15 million, for example.

Signings would be witnessed by a notary public, who would provide a code for payments. The notary public would be responsible for preventing any fraud.

Section VI.11. Selling on used cars

Transfers made to pay for used cars would detail the amount the car is worth, according to the model and year, etc. We would state the amount we wish to charge and the two current accounts involved. Details would not be required as the Department of Motor Vehicles would have a system for reading the digital fingerprints of both the buyer and the seller. Used car salesmen would use their company cards.

The buyer would pay the purchase tax.

 Payments would be made in full.

Section VI.12. Maintenance fees and property tax

Unless paid by direct debit, building maintenance fees would be paid by going in person to the relevant bank and paying by fingerprint, as banks would also use the fingerprint machine payment system.

If our bank was the same as that of the community bank account, the amount would be immediately subtracted from our balance. The bank would merely have to scan the barcode on the invoice.

To pay property tax, etc., the system would function in the same way.

These expenses could be deductible, such as maintenance fees for the building in which our office is located, or the office garage, for example.

Section VI.13. Buying property

Using black money would be strictly prohibited in order to prevent tax fraud.

Upon signing the deed, the notary public would send the data for the candidate to transfer the payment to a server which would generate a code.

The process would function like any other transfer, with the server producing a code which the notary public would record in the deed.

This system would be for upfront payments, however, with property to be bought over a period of 30 years, for example, involving a bank loan and therefore the bank making the transfer.

If paying upfront, we would initially see a debt registered to our account. We would then consult the code on the Central Computer website or on the deed itself and make the transfer.

Upon refreshing the system, the Central Computer would check that everything is correct, informing the Municipal Computer of our personal income and expenditure, and then the Central Computer.

If the transfer was unsuccessful, the Central Computer would be placed in contact with the notary public by means of an automatic email in order for the notary public to advise both parties. A period of time would, however, be given for the payment, such as a month.

Section VI.14. Churches

Churches would have many small payment machines, allowing us to enter the amount we wish to donate. Such donations would be capped at €50 per day, €300 per month, and €3,600 per year.

Amounts paid for lighting candles would be fixed, with the payment made by means of fingerprints or cards, including those used by politicians and minors.

Large sums of money for charities or NGOs would not be donated by means of these machines, and would instead use bank transfer, without fixed limits. This would be the same for political parties, whose accounts can be viewed by any server, with tax benefits. The Central Computer would register such benefits, with this information useful for personal tax declarations.

Section VI.15. Donations to cancer charities

Such donations would be made by means of a special payment machine like those used in churches, whereby we would state the amount to be donated, with this registered on a server and the amount then entering the current account of the cancer association.

The same would happen for non-profit organizations, which would provide us with receipts stating the money donated.

Section VI.16. Clothing stores

Clothing items would feature labels showing the price and allowing us to pay by means of our fingerprint or company card. Politicians' and minors' cards could also be used.

Clothing items could be returned within 15 days for small items, or within 30 days for larger items, with the store updating its stock totals.

In the case of exchanges for another size, a new purchase would be made, charging us the difference, and with the store updating its stock totals.

In the case of returns, the number on the receipt would be used to assign a purchase of €0 and this used to refund our money, as the Central Computer would pick up on two receipts with the same number and file the second one worth €0.

Section VI.17. Book stores and newsstands

All books have an ISBN code, which payment machines would scan in order to know the genre, meaning once we have scanned our fingerprint or card for payment, a receipt would be issued with the name of the book and the cost of the purchase.

It would be convenient for all items sold in newsstands to have bar-codes in order for the system to be the same as the one used in book stores.

Newspapers would have barcodes.

Candy stores would feature codes on boxes of candy, registering the quantity sold.

Section VI.18. Private classes

The maximum income generated from private classes would be €300 per month, as otherwise drugs could be sold under such a front or illegal transfers made.

In the case of private classes administered to minors, a family member would make a series of transfers which would not exceed €50 per day. Adults would pay for their own classes by means of bank transfers.

Section VI.19. Caring for the elderly

This kind of care would be covered by an association dedicated to finding carers work, functioning like a normal company, with the association using its own payment machines.

A salary of up to €300 per month could be charged without the need to belong to an association.

Section VI.20. Domestic staff and cleaners

These kinds of professionals would also belong to an association, which would search for jobs and use its own payment machine. Earnings of under €300 per month would not be taxed and could be used to help pay bills.

When paying, the company would indicate the various items purchased with the company card, whether cleaning items, food, or labor. They would also pay social security.

Section VI.21. Fines

The Department of Motor Vehicles would charge drivers automatically by means of payment machines.

If a fine were issued due to speeding caught on speed camera, a letter would be sent out for drivers to identify themselves. This could be done online by means of a code written in the letter, or in person at the department itself.

Upon confirmation of our ID, the department would charge us by means of our international ID number.

If unable to pay our fine, we would use the current procedures, with a timeframe used for payment. When the period expires, the system would be refreshed, and if we still don't have money, our car would be repossessed.

Section VI.22. Soccer players

Salaries would be established for soccer players, which would be communicated to the Central Computer, along with any bonuses paid for wins or draws.

An exception would be made for star soccer players and other celebrities from the worlds of sport, politics, and business, meaning no ceiling for their earnings would be set.

Income made by clubs in Champions League soccer games would also be monitored.

Black money would be eliminated, such as the infamous bonuses paid out for winning or losing.

All of the illegal activities committed by FIFA and UEFA would be eradicated.

Section VI.23. The stock market

The stock market would operate the same way as it does now, with shares sold and bought by means of banks. All our wins and losses would be communicated to the Central Computer.

This information would be communicated to the accounting system in the Central Computer, in order to be factored into our personal tax declaration, charging us if applicable.

Section VI.24. Problems with supermarkets and department stores

Prices in supermarkets and hypermarkets would not be updated by payment machines, but instead by the company's own computers, as prices would fluctuate due to the various offers.

The computers would be connected to all the various payment machines, communicating the costs of the different items.

These computers would have a database with all of the customer data, as people may pay at different cash registers on different days. Any of these cash registers would be able to identify us as regular or new customers.

Cashiers would also charge us for items such as meat, produce, and fish, etc, which may be from a separate unit located in the hypermarket. They would automatically know how much to charge us upon uploading the item.

This would be performed by means of the hypermarket's computer program, transferring the money to the produce or meat section, etc., which may have a different corporate tax number than the store but charge for items under the same system.

Some hypermarkets sell goods stocked by another company, for which a rent is paid. The hypermarket would then pay the company for their products, with expired products removed by the company and the money refunded. This would all be performed by means of the hypermarket's payment machines.

Minors would be able to purchase any items except alcohol and tobacco.

Section VI.25. Shared apartments

Rent shared by roommates would be paid by means of bank transfer, although they would then have to take turns to go to the supermarket. Normally such rent does not exceed €300 per month, as this would be prohibited by the system, therefore turns would have to be taken.

Section VI.26. Hire purchases

For this kind of sale, the Central Computer would need to know the number of installments to be made, with the payment machine registering the number and sending it to a server in the system.

The Central Computer would charge the money each month, transferring it to the company's bank account. If we were to run out of money, the company would be informed by means of an automatically generated email, advising the company to initiate the relevant legal proceedings.

Section VI.27. Drugstores

Payment machines in drugstores would be different due to the copay schemes whereby drugs are free or charged at 10% or 40%, etc. If our medication is not free, then we would pay by means of fingerprint payment (with company and politicians' cards invalid), along with the corresponding part by the relevant body.

The server would be informed of what we paid by means of our fingerprint and the quantity to be paid by the administrative body, which the drugstore would always charge.

The payment machine used in drugstores would also have a list of drugs not covered by social security.

Uploading a prescription to the system would be attached with a code which could only be uploaded once, preventing drugstores from uploading the same prescription multiple times and committing fraud.

Section VI.28. Freelancers

This section covers dentists, plumbers, lawyers, attorneys, notary publics, estate agents, and doctors, etc.

Such professionals would use payment machines registering the items to be charged. For those in the legal sphere, limits would also be set by means of a maximum threshold charged for procedures such as divorce or theft, etc.

As may be gauged, this issue is complicated. Upon implementing the system, a study would have to be launched into the nuances of the various professions, as architects and surveyors charge through their association on a project-by-project basis.

CHAPTER VII

Capitalism under our system

Finally, it must be stated that corporations would function very well under our system, once the current rampant tax fraud has been eradicated. The capitalist model is the best existing model, as it has been demonstrated to produce less poverty.

Our computer system would benefit right-wing politicians supportive of free dismissal, which would in turn benefit companies, spurring labor reform. It would also benefit left-wing politicians who are against cuts and in favor of better welfare such as decent unemployment benefits.

I haven't provided much financial data, as this can be contradictory, varying between the various media outlets and economists. Nobody has categorically stated that the big solution is to get rid of tax fraud, instead focusing on the inefficient strategy of using tax inspectors.

My opinion on tax inspectors is that they can be bribed, meaning inspections by means of computers are a more secure option.

I do believe in the approximate figure given for tax fraud, because many media outlets seem to be in agreement. The source of such fraud is, however, what I would question, as some say it stems from large companies and multinationals, and others from freelancers and small and medium-sized companies. My personal opinion is that it is somewhere in the middle, as Aristotle would say. I don't think that 20% of the economy is responsible for 75% of its tax fraud.

Such tax fraud must also be added to social security fraud, as in Spain 25% of the economy is underground, which would disappear under the use of our computer system.

Fiber-optic networks now cover the entire planet, demonstrating that the technology required to implement our system is in place.

Under the perfect capitalist system outlined in this book, people would live better and would be happier, and as it states in the US Constitution, every individual has the right to the pursuit of happiness.

PROLOGE   3

CHARPTER I. El system   8
Section I.1. A description of the system, its one great trick, and
            Why this doesn't necessarily spell the end for cash   8
Section I.2. The current systems   9
Section I.3. Other systems and several problems with our own   10
Section I.4. System advantages   10
Section I.5. How to prevent kidnappings   11
Section I.6. How to greatly reduce theft   12
Section I.7. How to minimize political corruption   13
Section I.9. How to reduce crime   14
Section I.10. How to prevent smuggling   14
Section I.11. Police   14
Section I.12. Tackling drug trafficking   15
Section I.13. How to prevent illegal immigration   16
Section I.14. Anti-terrorism measures   18
Section I.15. Our system and security   19
Section I.16. The Central Computer, electronic money, and
             the bunker   20
Section I.17. Operation methods   21
Section I.18. Children, teenagers, and death   22
Section I.19. Traveling abroad   24
Section I.20. Problems with foreigners remaining in other countries   25
Section I.21. Transfers between individuals, banks, and companies   25
Section I.22. The payment system for freelancers and employees   27
Section I.23. PayPal and other online payment systems   29
Section I.24. The main problem with our system   30

CHAPTER II. Technology   31
Section II.1. Payment machines   31
Section II.2. Invoices and receipts   32
Section II.3. How to prevent war breaking out between banks   32
Section II.4. The different types of payment machines   32
Section II.5. The Central Computer and the servers   34

Section II.6. Servers and standing data 34

Section II.7. Tricks for improving the system 35

Section II.8. The Central Computer's robot system 37

Section II.9. Fingerprints 41

Section II.10. Empty bank accounts 42

Section II.11. The Central Computer and transfers 42

Section II.12. Situations which may result in system delays
      and solutions 44

CHAPTER III. The sophisticated system 47

Section III.1. Description and advantages 47

Section III.2. Municipal Computers 47

Section III.3. System operations within a single country and
      duplicate data 49

Section III.4. Our programs and those used by the system 49

Section III.5. False invoices and receipts 50

Section III.6. The system in the European Union 50

Section III.7. How to prevent fraud 51

Section III.8. The 100% sophisticated system 51

Section III.9. Stolen and destroyed goods and how to prevent
      fraud 53

Section III.10. Imports and exports 53

Section III.11. The consultations and their technology 55

CHAPTER IV. The bunker 57

CHAPTER V. The economy 59

Section V.1. The system, its investigative activities, and automatic
      tax declarations 59

Section V.2. Companies' maximum and minimum profit thresholds 61

Section V.3. Businesses and debt 62

Section V.4. Modules 63

Section V.5. Deductible items and VAT 63

Section V.6. Reserve funds and politicians' allowances 65

Section V.7. When is bookkeeping performed? 66

Section V.8. Personal Income Tax   66
Section V.9. The national bank, the Public Treasury, and the
           councils.   67
Section V.10. Under our system, everyone would get paid   67
Section V.11. How to eliminate debt, using Spain as an example   69

CHAPTER VI. How the various businesses would run under
           our system   **73**
Section VI.1. Slot machines   73
Section VI.2. Cigarette machines   74
Section VI.3. Vending machines   74
Section VI.4. Shows and sporting events   74
Section VI.5. Bank commission   75
Section VI.6. How to sell on our jewelry and stamps, etc.   75
Section VI.7. Casinos, unregulated gambling, and betting   76
Section VI.8. The lottery, betting on sports, bingo, and horseracing 76
Section VI.9. Collect on delivery   77
Section VI.10. Soccer transfers   77
Section VI.11. Selling on used cars   78
Section VI.12. Maintenance fees and property tax   78
Section VI.13. Buying property   79
Section VI.14. Churches   79
Section VI.15. Donations to cancer charities   80
Section VI.16. Clothing stores   80
Section VI.17. Book stores and newsstands   80
Section VI.18. Private classes   81
Section VI.19. Caring for the elderly   81
Section VI.20. Domestic staff and cleaners   81
Section VI.21. Fines   82
Section VI.22. Soccer players   82
Section VI.23. The stock market   83
Section VI.24. Problems with supermarkets and department stores   83
Section VI.25. Shared apartments   84
Section VI.26. Hire purchases   84
Section VI.27. Drugstores   84

Section VI.28. Freelancers 85

CHAPTER VII. Capitalism under our system 87